Disclaimer

The publisher of this book is by no way associated with the National Institute of Standards and Technology (NIST). The NIST did not publish this book. It was published by 50 page publications under the public domain license.

50 Page Publications.

Book Title: A User's Guide for FAST: Engineering Tools for Estimating Fire Growth and Smoke Transport

Book Author: Richard D. Peacock; Paul A. Reneke; Walter W. Jones; Richard W. Bukowski; Glenn P. Forney;

Book Abstract: FAST is a collection of fire modeling tools which uses the underlying fire model CFAST and adds the routines of FIREFORM to provide engineering calculations of fire phenomena in compartmented structures. This manual provides documentation and examples for using FAST. It describes how to install the software on a computer and provides a guide for the use of FAST using examples.

Citation: NIST SP - 921

Keyword: computer models; computer programs; evacuation; fire models; fire research; hazard assessment; human behavior; toxicity

U.S. DEPARTMENT OF COMMERCE

TECHNOLOGY ADMINISTRATION

National Institute of Standards and Technology

Special Publication 921
2000 Edition

A User's Guide for FAST: Engineering Tools for Estimating Fire Growth and Smoke Transport

Richard D. Peacock
Paul A. Reneke
Walter W. Jones
Richard W. Bukowski
Glenn P. Forney

Special Publication 921
2000 Edition

A User's Guide for FAST: Engineering Tools for Estimating Fire Growth and Smoke Transport

Richard D. Peacock
Paul A. Reneke
Walter W. Jones
Richard W. Bukowski
Glenn P. Forney

National Institute of Standards and Technology
Building and Fire Research Laboratory
Gaithersburg, MD 20899

January 2000

U.S. Department of Commerce
William M. Daley, *Secretary*
Technology Administration
Gary R. Bachula, *Acting Under Secretary for Technology*
National Institute of Standards and Technology
Raymond G. Kammer, *Director*

National Institute of Standards
and Technology
Special Publication 921
Natl. Inst. Stand. Technol.
Spec. Publ.
192 pages (January 2000)
CODEN: NSPUE2

U.S. Government Printing Office
Washington: 2000

For sale by the Superintendent
of Documents
U.S. Government Printing Office
Washington, DC 20402-9325

Bibliographic Information

Abstract

FAST is a collection of fire modeling tools which uses the underlying fire model CFAST and adds the routines of FIREFORM to provide engineering calculations of fire phenomena in compartmented structures. This manual provides documentation and examples for using FAST. It describes how to install the software on a computer and provides a guide for the use of FAST using examples.

Keywords

Computer models; computer programs; evacuation; fire models; fire research; hazard assessment; human behavior; toxicity

Ordering Information

National Institute of Standards and Technology
Special Publication 921
Natl. Inst. Stand. Technol.
Spec. Publ.
192 pages (November 1997)
CODEN: NSPUE2

U.S. Government Printing Office
Washington: 2000

For sale by the Superintendent of Documents
U.S. Government Printing Office
Washington, DC 20402-9325

DISCLAIMER

The U. S. Department of Commerce makes no warranty, expressed or implied, to users of FAST and associated computer programs, and accepts no responsibility for its use. Users of FAST assume sole responsibility under Federal law for determining the appropriateness of its use in any particular application; for any conclusions drawn from the results of its use; and for any actions taken or not taken as a result of analyzes performed using these tools.

Users are warned that FAST is intended for use only by those competent in the field of fire safety and is intended only to supplement the informed judgment of the qualified user. The software package is a computer model which may or may not have predictive value when applied to a specific set of factual circumstances. Lack of accurate predictions by the model could lead to erroneous conclusions with regard to fire safety. All results should be evaluated by an informed user.

INTENT AND USE

The algorithms, procedures, and computer programs described in this report constitute a methodology for predicting some of the consequences resulting from a specified fire. They have been compiled from the best knowledge and understanding currently available, but have important limitations that must be understood and considered by the user. The program is intended for use by persons competent in the field of fire safety and with some familiarity with personal computers. It is intended as an aid in the fire safety decision-making process.

A User's Guide for FAST: Engineering Tools for Estimating Fire Growth and Smoke Transport

Richard D. Peacock, Paul A. Reneke, Walter W. Jones,
Richard W. Bukowski, and Glenn P. Forney

Building and Fire Research Laboratory
National Institute of Standards and Technology

1 Introduction

Simple algebraic equations have been a mainstay of engineering calculations for as long as they have existed. In 1984 Bukowski suggested that a *series* of separate calculations of fire phenomena could be used to evaluate a complex, interactive process, i.e., a fire hazard analysis [1]. A broader series of equations applicable to fire growth estimates was also published in 1985 [2]. Nelson [3] extended this concept further with FIREFORM and FPEtool to provide simple models along with engineering calculations in a software package that is widely used for fire safety engineering calculations. In June 1989, the Center for Fire Research (now part of the Building and Fire Research Laboratory) at the National Institute of Standards and Technology released a method for quantifying the hazards to occupants of buildings from fires, and the relative contribution of specific products (e.g., furniture, wire insulation) to those hazards [4], [5]. The culmination of 6 years of development this method, called HAZARD I, was the first such comprehensive application of fire modeling in the world. It combined criteria based on expert judgment and calculations to estimate the consequences of a specified fire.

FAST is a collection of procedures which builds on the computer model CFAST [6] to provide engineering estimates of fire hazard in compartmented structures. It is the successor to the earlier software HAZARD I, and FASTLite [7] for use in fire hazard calculations. FAST includes individual engineering calculations based on those included in FIREFORM, an updated version of the fire model CFAST (an earlier version of which was part of HAZARD I and FASTLite), and a new user interface similar to that used in FASTLite. This manual provides documentation and examples for using FAST. It describes how to install the software on your computer and provides a guide for the use of FAST.

At the outset, it is important to note that FAST is intended for use only by those competent in the field of fire safety and is intended only to supplement the informed judgment of the qualified user. The software is intended to provide quantitative estimates of some of the likely consequences of a fire. The model has been subjected to a range of verification tests to assess the accuracy of the calculations. Like any computer calculation however, the quality of the calculated result is directly related to the quality of the inputs provided by the user. Lack of accurate predictions by the model could lead to erroneous conclusions with regard to fire safety. All results should be evaluated by an informed user.

1.1 Getting Started

FAST is intended to be a tool to allow estimation of fire spread in buildings. The software and documentation included on the distribution CD ROM can be installed by following the instructions included with the CD ROM. Although installation of the software is intended to be simple and one can have the software "up and running" quickly, efficient use of all of the features of the software necessitates reading the documentation. The user is advised to begin this process by scanning the table of contents to become familiar with the contents of the manual.

1.1.1 Learning FAST

Developing appropriate inputs for a realistic simulation of typical fire scenarios can be imposing. While typical values are supplied for much of the information, nearly all of the data can be customized for each specific test case. Details of all of these inputs are included in this document. This section provides a possible strategy to guide one through the documentation.

1.   Section 1.2 on page 5 provides a general description of the theoretical basis of FAST along with a summary of the limitations of the predictive equations used in FAST.

2.   Beginning on page 14, there is a detailed description of each element of the user interface from using a mouse and keyboard with the software to each type of display used for input of data and presentation of results for the model. For some users, this section will be a review. For others, some study will be required to become familiar with the concepts of a graphical user interface.

3.   Section 2, on page 23, begins with a simple example of a fire in a single compartment and provides a step-by step guide to running this example. Reviewing this example will familiarize the user with the basic operation of the software.

4.   Section 5, on page 83, describes a number of estimation tools which are included with FAST and can be used to provide estimates of individual fire phenomena. While some of these tools require more detail than a couple of input variables, most routines require relatively little effort to obtain an estimate.

5.   Finally, refer to section 2.2 on page 25, for a detailed description of each of the inputs for FAST which can be used to customize an individual test case.

1.1.2 Hardware and Software Requirements

- A 386 or later IBM* compatible PC with at least 4 megabytes of free extended memory. FAST does not run on 8086 or 80286 microcomputers.

- At least a VGA compatible graphics display. The installation program automatically determines video hardware for each installation and sets the software accordingly.

- The mouse driver must be 100 percent MS-mouse compatible. If problems are experienced, such as the mouse not responding within the user interface, check to be certain the mouse driver was loaded when the computer was turned on. If the driver was loaded and problems persist, update the version of the driver software by contacting the manufacturer of the mouse. For operation in a DOS box in Windows 95, a separate mouse drive is not required.

- Do not run memory resident (TSR) programs that were originally developed for 8086 platforms while trying to run FAST. Older TSR applications may not take advantage of EMS and XMS memory use and can cause operating system conflicts with the newer technology in graphics displays and interfaces.

1.1.3 Installation

An installation program which prompts for the necessary information and copies the necessary files onto a hard disk is included on the distribution CD ROM. FAST is a DOS-based program and should be installed directly from the DOS prompt. If necessary, exit MS-Windows or any menuing software prior to installation.

To install FAST on a PC computer system, place the CD ROM into the drive (typically DOS drive D:) and enter the following DOS command:

```
D:INSTALL
```

---

* The use of company or trade names within this report is made solely for the purpose of identifying those computer hardware or software products operationally compatible with FAST. Such use does not constitute any endorsement by NIST.

3

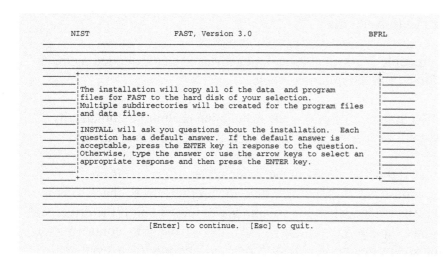

```
    NIST                    FAST, Version 3.0                    BFRL
_____
_____
_____+-----------------------------------------------------------+____
_____|                                                           |____
_____|The installation will copy all of the data  and program    |____
_____|files for FAST to the hard disk of your selection.         |____
_____|Multiple subdirectories will be created for the program files|____
_____|and data files.                                            |____
_____|                                                           |____
_____|INSTALL will ask you questions about the installation.  Each|____
_____|question has a default answer.  If the default answer is    |____
_____|acceptable, press the ENTER key in response to the question.|____
_____|Otherwise, type the answer or use the arrow keys to select an|____
_____|appropriate response and then press the ENTER key.          |____
_____|                                                           |____
_____+-----------------------------------------------------------+____
_____
_____
_____
                  [Enter] to continue.  [Esc] to quit.
```

If your computer is configured so that the CD ROM drive is assigned a drive letter other than D:, replace the D: in the command above with the appropriate drive letter. Several questions are asked about the computer system and how and where to install the modules. Answer none, some, or all of the questions as appropriate for your specific needs. Usually, the defaults provided by the installation program are sufficient. On several of the screens, prompts are provided to fill in information or change the defaults suggested by the installation module if necessary. These screens are described in more detail below.

FAST is installed in a single subdirectory structure on a hard disk. The first two screens prompt for the drive letter of the hard disk (usually C:), and the name of the main program directory (where the actual software is installed). For most installations, the defaults are sufficient provided the drive selected contains at least 12 megabytes of free space. For custom installations, any drive containing at least 12 megabytes of free space may be selected. Any valid nonexistent directory may be used for the program directory.

```
    NIST                    FAST, Version 3.0                    BFRL
_____
_____
_____
_____+-----------------------------------------------+_____
_____|                                               |_____
_____|Installing file:                               |_____
_____|C:\CFAST\CFAST.EXE                             |_____
_____|                                               |_____
_____|              41%                              |_____
_____|  _____  |_____
_____|                                               |_____
_____+-----------------------------------------------+_____
_____
_____
_____
_____
_____
                        [Esc] to quit.
```

As the files are copied from the installation CD ROM to the hard disk, the installation program shows the progress on the screen.

In order to operate correctly, the installation module may need to create or modify the FILES= statement in the DOS startup file CONFIG.SYS. If you wish to modify the file yourself, you may skip this step. The FILES= statement must specify a minimum of 50 files for the software to operate correctly.

4

1.2 Overview and Limitations

Analytical models for predicting fire behavior have been evolving since the 1960's. Over the past 3 decades, the completeness of the models has grown. In the beginning, the focus of these efforts was to describe in mathematical language the various phenomena which were observed in fire growth, spread, and extinction. These separate representations have typically described only a small part of the fire phenomena needed for safety analysis. The combination of multiple individual phenomena can create a complex computer code intended to give an estimate of the expected course of a fire based upon given input parameters. These analytical models have progressed to the point of providing predictions of fire behavior with an accuracy suitable for most engineering applications. In a recent international survey [8], 36 actively supported models were identified. Of these, 20 predict the fire generated environment (mainly temperature) and 19 predict smoke movement in some way. Six calculate fire growth rate, nine predict fire endurance, four address detector or sprinkler response, and two calculate evacuation times. The computer models now available vary considerably in scope, complexity, and purpose. Simple "room filling" models such as the Available Safe Egress Time (ASET) model [9] run quickly on almost any computer, and provide good estimates of a few parameters of interest for a fire in a single compartment. A special purpose model provides a single function or facility. For example, COMPF2 [10] calculates post-flashover room temperatures and LAVENT [11] includes the interaction of ceiling jets with fusible links in a compartment containing ceiling vents and draft curtains. Very detailed models like the HARVARD 5 code [12] or FIRST [13] predict the burning behavior of multiple items in a single room, along with the time-dependent conditions therein.

In addition to the single-room models mentioned above, there are a smaller number of multi-room models which have been developed. These include the BRI transport model [14], the HARVARD 6 code [15] (which is a multi-room version of HARVARD 5), FAST [16], CCFM [17], CFAST [18], and FASTLite [7].

Although the papers are several years old, Mitler [19] and Jones [20] reviewed the underlying physics in several of the fire models in detail. The models fall into two categories: those that start with the principles of conservation of mass, momentum, and energy; the other type typically are curve fits to particular experiments or series of experiments, used in order to try and tease out the underlying relationship among some parameters. In both cases, errors arise in those instances where a mathematical short cut was taken, a simplifying assumption was made, or something important was not well enough understood to include.

Once a mathematical representation of the underlying fire physics has been developed, the conservation equations can be re-cast into predictive equations for temperature, smoke and gas concentration, and other parameters of interest, and are coded into a computer for solution. The environment in a fire is constantly changing. Thus the equations are usually in the form of *differential equations*. A complete set of equations can compute the conditions produced by the fire at a given time in a specified volume of air. Referred to as a *control volume*, the model assumes that the predicted conditions within this volume are uniform at any time. Thus, the control volume has one temperature, smoke density, gas concentration, etc.

Different models divide the building into different numbers of control volumes depending on the desired level of detail. The most common fire model, known as a *zone model*, generally uses two control volumes to describe a room – an upper layer and a lower layer. In the room with the fire, additional control volumes for the fire plume or the ceiling jet may be included to improve the accuracy of the prediction.

This two-layer approach has evolved from observation of such layering in real-scale fire experiments. Hot gases collect at the ceiling and fill the room from the top. While these experiments show some variation in conditions within the layer, these are small compared to the differences between the layers. Thus, the zone model can produce a fairly realistic simulation under most conditions.

Other types of models include *network models* and *field models*. The former use one element per room and are used to predict conditions in spaces far removed from the fire room, where temperatures are near ambient and layering does not occur. The field model goes to the other extreme, dividing the room into thousands or even hundreds of thousands of grid points. Such models can predict the variation in conditions within the layers, but typically require far longer run times than zone models. Thus, they are used when highly detailed calculations are desired.

1.2.1 Applicability of the Fire Model

The CFAST model used in FAST is a two-zone model used to calculate the evolving distribution of smoke and fire gases and the temperature throughout a building during a fire. CFAST is based on solving a set of equations that predict state variables (pressure, temperature and so on) based on the enthalpy and mass flux over small increments of time. These equations are derived from the conservation equations for energy mass, and momentum, and the ideal gas law. These conservation equations are always correct, everywhere. Thus any errors which might be made by the model cannot come from these equations, but rather come from the numerical representation of the equations and from simplifying assumptions.

The CFAST model has been subjected to a wide range of comparisons to experimental data. The comparisons range from simple single-compartment fires [21], multiple compartments on a single floor [22], a seven-story hotel [22], to large aircraft hangers [23], [24]. For variables deemed of interest to the user of the model, the CFAST model provided predictions of the magnitude and trends (time to critical conditions and general curve shape) for the experiments which range in quality from within a few percent to a factor of two to three of the measured values. While CFAST has been successfully used in a wide range of applications, it is impossible to provided exact limits on the use of the model. Rather, the user should be familiar with the underlying fire physics in the model, typical uses of the model available in the literature, and the limitations of the model.

1.2.2 Fires

Within CFAST, a fire is a source of fuel which is released at a specified rate. This fuel is converted into enthalpy (the conversion factor is the heat of combustion) and mass (the conversion factor is the yield of a particular species) as it burns. Burning can take place in the portion of the plume in the lower layer (if any), in the upper layer, or in a door jet. For an unconstrained fire, the burning will all take place within the fire plume. For a constrained fire, burning will take place where there is sufficient oxygen. Where insufficient oxygen is entrained into the fire plume, unburned fuel will successively move into and burn in: the upper layer of the fire room, the plume in the doorway to the next room, the upper layer of the next room, the plume in the doorway to the third room, and so forth until it is consumed or gets to the outside.

This version of CFAST includes the ability to track, independently, multiple fires in one or more rooms of the building. These fires are treated as totally separate entities, i.e., with no interaction of the plumes or radiative exchange between fires in a room.

Like all current zone fire models, this version of CFAST does not include a pyrolysis model to predict fire growth. Rather pyrolysis rates for each fire modeled define the fire history. The similarity of that input to the real fire problem of interest will determine the accuracy of the resulting calculation. The user must account for any interactions between the fire and the pyrolysis rate.

1.2.3 Plumes and Layers

Above any burning object, a plume is formed which is not considered to be a part of either layer, but which acts as a pump for enthalpy and mass from the lower layer into the upper layer (upward only). For the fire plume, CFAST uses an empirical correlation to determine the amount of mass moved between layers by the plume.

Two sources exist for moving enthalpy and mass between the layers within and between rooms. Within the room, the fire plume provides one source. The other source of mixing between the layers occurs at vents such as doors or windows. Here, there is mixing at the boundary of the opposing flows moving into and out of the room. The degree of mixing is based on an empirically derived mixing relation. Both the outflow and inflow entrain air from the surrounding layers. The flow at vents is also modeled as a plume (called the door plume or jet), and uses the same equations as the fire plume, with two differences. First, an offset is calculated to account for entrainment within the doorway and second, the equations are modified to account for the rectangular geometry of vents compared to the round geometry of fire plumes. All plumes within the simulation entrain air from their surroundings according to an empirically derived entrainment relation. Entrainment of relatively cool, non smoke laden air adds oxygen to the plume and allows burning of the fuel. It also causes it to expand as the plume moves upward in the shape of an inverted cone. The entrainment in a vent is caused by bi-directional flow. It is not exactly the same as a normal plume, so some error arises when this entrainment is approximated by a normal plume entrainment algorithm.

While experiments show that there is very little mixing between the layers at their interface, sources of convection such as radiators or diffusers of heating and air conditioning systems, and the downward flows of gases caused by cooling at walls, will cause such mixing. These are examples of phenomena which are not included because the theories are still under development. Also, the plumes are *assumed* not to be affected by other flows which may occur. For example, experiments show that if the burning object is near the door the strong inflow of air will cause the plume axis to lean away from the door and affect entrainment of gases into the plume. Such effects are not included in the model.

As discussed above, each room is divided into two layers, the upper and lower. At the start of the simulation, the layers in each room are initialized at ambient conditions and by default, the upper layer volume set to 0.001 of the room volume (an arbitrary, small value set to avoid the potential mathematical problems associated with dividing by zero). Other values can be set. As enthalpy and mass are pumped into the upper layer by the fire plume, the upper layer expands in volume causing the lower layer to decrease in volume and the interface to move downward. If the door to the next room has a soffit, there can be no flow through the vent from the upper layer until the interface reaches the bottom of that soffit. Thus in the early stages the expanding upper layer will push down on the lower layer air and force it into the next compartment through the vent by expansion.

Once the interface reaches the soffit level, a door plume forms and flow from the fire room to the next room is initiated. As hot gas flows from the fire room to fill the second room, the lower layer of air in the second room is pushed down. As a result, some of this air flows into the fire room through the lower part of the connecting doorway (or vent). Thus, a vent between the fire room and connecting rooms can have simultaneous, opposing flows of air. All flows are driven by pressure differences and density differences that result from temperature differences and layer depths. Thus the key to getting the right flows is to correctly distribute the fire's mass and enthalpy between the layers.

1.2.4 Vent Flow

Flow through vents is the dominant phenomenon in a fire model because it fluctuates most rapidly and transfers the greatest amount of enthalpy on an instantaneous basis of all the source terms. Also, it is most sensitive to changes in the environment. Flow through vents comes in two varieties. The first we refer to as horizontal flow. It is the flow which is normally thought of in discussing fires. It encompasses flow through doors, windows and so on. The other is vertical flow and can occur if there is a hole in the ceiling or floor of a compartment. This latter phenomena is particularly important in two disparate situations: a ship, and buildings with manual or automatic heat and smoke venting.

Flow through normal vents is governed by the pressure difference across a vent. There are two situations which give rise to flow through vents. The first, and usually thought of in fire problems, is that of air or smoke which is driven from a compartment by buoyancy. The second type of flow is due to expansion which is particularly important when conditions in the fire environment are changing rapidly. Rather than depending entirely on density differences between the two gases, the flow is forced by volumetric expansion.

Atmospheric pressure is about 100 000 Pa, fires produce pressure changes from 1 Pa to 1000 Pa and mechanical ventilation systems typically involve pressure differentials of about 1 Pa to 100 Pa. In order to solve these interactions correctly, we must be able to follow pressure differences of ≈ 0.1 Pa out of 100 000 Pa for the overall problem, or 10^{-4} Pa for adjacent compartments.

1.2.5 Heat Transfer

Heat transfer is the mechanism by which the gas layers exchange energy with their surroundings. Convective transfer occurs from the layers to the room surfaces. The enthalpy thus transferred in the simulations conducts through the wall, ceiling, or floor in the direction perpendicular to the surface only. CFAST is more advanced than most models in this field since it allows different material properties to be used for the ceiling, floor, and walls of each room (although all the walls of a room must be the same). Additionally, CFAST uniquely allows each surface to be composed of up to three distinct layers for each surface, which are treated separately in the conduction calculation. This not only produces more accurate results, but allows the user to deal naturally with the actual building construction. Material thermophysical properties are *assumed* to be constant, although we know that they actually vary with temperature. This assumption is made because data over the required temperature range is scarce even for common materials, and because the variation is relatively small for most materials. However the user should recognize that some materials may change mechanical properties with temperature. These effects are not modeled.

Radiative transfer occurs among the fire(s), gas layers and compartment surfaces (ceiling, walls and floor). This transfer is a function of the temperature differences and the emissivity of the gas layers as well as the compartment surfaces. For the fire and typical surfaces, emissivity values only vary over a small range. For the gas layers, however, the emissivity is a function of the concentration of species which are strong radiators: predominately smoke particulates, carbon dioxide, and water. Thus errors in the species concentrations can give rise to errors in the distribution of enthalpy among the layers, which results in errors in temperatures, resulting in errors in the flows. This illustrates just how tightly coupled the predictions made by CFAST can be.

9

1.2.6 Species Concentration and Deposition

When the layers are initialized at the start of the simulation, they are set to ambient conditions. These are the initial temperatures specified by the user, and 23 percent by mass (20.8 percent by volume) oxygen, 77 percent by mass (79 percent by volume) nitrogen, a mass concentration of water specified by the user as a relative humidity, and a zero concentration of all other species. As fuel is pyrolyzed, the various species are produced in direct relation to the mass of fuel burned (this relation is the species yield specified by the user for the fuel burning). Since oxygen is consumed rather than produced by the burning, the "yield" of oxygen is negative, and is set internally to correspond to the amount of oxygen needed to burn the fuel. Also, hydrogen cyanide and hydrogen chloride are assumed to be products of pyrolysis whereas carbon dioxide, carbon monoxide, water, and soot are products of combustion.

Each unit mass of a species produced is carried in the flow to the various rooms and accumulates in the layers. The model keeps track of the mass of each species in each layer, and knows the volume of each layer as a function of time. The mass divided by the volume is the mass concentration, which along with the molecular weight gives the concentration in volume percent or ppm as appropriate.

CFAST uses a combustion chemistry scheme different from any other model. While others compute each species concentration with an independent yield fraction, CFAST maintains a carbon-hydrogen-oxygen balance. The scheme is applied in three places. The first is burning in the portion of the plume which is in the lower layer of the room of fire origin. The second is the portion in the upper layer, also in the room of origin. The third is in the vent flow which entrains air from a lower layer into an upper layer in an adjacent compartment. This is equivalent to solving the conservation equations for each species independently.

1.2.7 Assumptions and Limitations

FAST consists of a collection of data and computer programs which are used to *simulate* the important time-dependent phenomena involved in fires. The major functions provided include calculation of:

- the production of enthalpy and mass (smoke and gases) by one or more burning objects in one room, based on small- or large-scale measurements,

- the buoyancy-driven as well as forced transport of this energy and mass through a series of specified rooms and connections (e.g., doors, windows, cracks, ducts),

- the resulting temperatures, smoke optical densities, and gas concentrations after accounting for heat transfer to surfaces and dilution by mixing with clean air.

As can be seen from this list, fire modeling involves an interdisciplinary consideration of physics, chemistry, fluid mechanics, and heat transfer. In some areas, fundamental laws (conservation of mass, energy, and momentum) can be used, whereas in others empirical correlations or even "educated guesses" must be employed to bridge gaps in existing knowledge. The necessary approximations required by operational practicality result in the introduction of uncertainties in the results. The user should understand the inherent assumptions and limitations of the programs, and use these programs judiciously – including sensitivity analyses for the ranges of values for key parameters – in order to make estimates of these uncertainties. This section provides an overview of these assumptions and limitations.

Specified Fire Limitations: An important limitation of the CFAST model is the absence of a fire growth model. At the present time, it is not practical to adapt currently available fire growth models for direct inclusion in CFAST. Therefore, the system utilizes a user specified fire, expressed in terms of time specified rates of energy and mass released by the burning item(s). Such data can be obtained by measurements taken in large- and small-scale calorimeters, or from room burns. Examples of their associated limitations are as follows:

1.   For a large-scale calorimeter, a product (e.g., chair, table, bookcase) is placed under a large collection hood and ignited by a 50 kW gas burner (simulating a wastebasket) placed adjacent to the item for 120 s. The combustion process then proceeds under assumed "free-burning" conditions, and the release rate data are measured. Potential sources of uncertainty here include measurement errors related to the instrumentation, and the degree to which "free-burning" conditions are not achieved (e.g., radiation from the gases under the hood or from the hood itself, and restrictions in the air entrained by the object causing locally reduced oxygen concentrations affecting the combustion chemistry). There are limited experimental data for upholstered furniture which suggest that prior to the onset of flashover in a compartment, the influence of the compartment on the burning behavior of the item is small. The differences obtained from the use of different types or locations of ignition sources have not been explored. These factors are discussed in reference [25].

2.   Where small-scale calorimeter data are used, procedures are available to extrapolate to the behavior of a full-size item. These procedures are based on empirical correlations of data which exhibit significant scatter, thus limiting their accuracy. For example, for upholstered furniture, the peak heat release rates estimated by the "triangular approximation" method averaged 91 percent (range 46 percent to 103 percent) of values measured for a group of 26 chairs with noncombustible frames, but only 63 perecnt (range 46 percent to 83 percent) of values measured for a group of 11 chairs with combustible frames [26]. Also, the triangle neglects the "tails" of the curve; these are the initial time from ignition to significant burning of the item, and the region of burning of the combustible frame, after the fabric and filler are consumed.

3.   The provided data and procedures only relate directly to burning of items initiated by relatively large flaming sources. Little data are currently available for release rates under

11

smoldering combustion, or for the high external flux and low oxygen conditions characteristic of post-flashover burning. While the model allows multiple items burning simultaneously, it does not account for the synergy of such multiple fires. Thus, for other ignition scenarios, multiple items burning simultaneously (which exchange energy by radiation and convection), combustible interior finish, and post-flashover conditions, the model can give estimates which are often nonconservative (the actual release rates would be *greater* than estimated). At present, the only sure way to account for all of these complex phenomena is to conduct a full-scale room burn and use the pyrolysis rates directly.

Zone Model and Transport Limitations: The basic assumption of all zone fire models is that each room can be divided into a small number of control volumes, each of which is internally uniform in temperature and composition. In CFAST, all rooms have two zones except the fire room, which has additional zones for the fire plume and ceiling jet, which are calculated separately to account for mass and heat transfer between the zones and between the zones and compartment surfaces. The boundary between the two layers in a room is called the interface.

It has generally been observed that in the spaces close to the fire, buoyantly stratified layers form. While in an experiment the temperature can be seen to vary within a given layer, these variations are small compared to the temperature difference between the layers.

Beyond the basic zone assumptions, the model typically involves a mixture of established theory (e.g., conservation equations), empirical correlations where there are data but no theory (e.g., flow and entrainment coefficients), and approximations where there are neither (e.g., post-flash-over combustion chemistry) or where their effect is considered secondary compared to the "cost" of inclusion. An example of a widely used assumption is that the estimated error from ignoring the variation of the thermal properties of structural materials with temperature is small. While this information would be fairly simple to add to the computer code, data are scarce over a broad range of temperatures even for the most common materials.

With a highly complex model such as CFAST, the only reasonable method of assessing impacts of assumptions and limitations is through the verification process, which is ongoing at the Building and Fire Research Laboratory (BFRL). Until the results of this process are available, the user should be aware of the general limits of zone modeling and some specific manifestations in CFAST. These include the following:

1.   Burning can be constrained by the available oxygen. However, this "constrained fire" (a "type 2" fire, see page 23) is not subject to the influences of radiation to enhance its burning rate, but is influenced by the oxygen available in the room. If a large mass loss rate is entered, the model will follow this input until there is insufficient oxygen available for that quantity of fuel to burn in the room. The unburned fuel (sometimes called excess pyrolyzate) is tracked as it flows out in the door jet, where it can entrain more oxygen. If this mixture is within the user-specified flammable range, it burns in the door plume. If

not, it will be tracked throughout the building until it eventually collects as unburned fuel or burns in a vent. The enthalpy released in the fire room and in each vent, as well as the total enthalpy released, is detailed in the output of the model. Since mass and enthalpy are conserved, the total will be correct. However, since combustion did not take place adjacent to the burning object, the actual mass burned could be lower than that specified by the user. The difference will be the unburned fuel.

2.   An oxygen combustion chemistry scheme is employed only in constrained (type 2 and greater) fires. Here user-specified hydrocarbon ratios and species yields are used by the model to predict concentrations. A balance among hydrogen, carbon, and oxygen molecules is maintained. Under some conditions, low oxygen or high temperature can change the combustion chemistry, with an attendant increase in the yields of products of incomplete combustion such as CO. Guidance is provided on how to adjust the CO/CO_2 ratio. However, not enough is known about these chemical processes to build this relationship into the model at the present time. Data in recent studies of CO generation in fires (e.g., reference [27], [28], and [29]) can assist in making such determinations.

3.   The entrainment coefficients are empirically determined values. Small errors in these values will have a small effect on the fire plume or the flow in the plume of gases exiting the door of that room. In a multi-compartment model such as CFAST, however, small errors in each door plume are multiplicative as the flow proceeds through many compartments, possibly resulting in a significant error in the furthest rooms. The data available from validation experiments [30] indicate that the values for entrainment coefficients currently used in most zone models produce good agreement for a three-compartment configuration. More data are needed for larger numbers of rooms to study this further.

4.   The only mechanisms provided in zone models to move enthalpy and mass into the upper layer of a room are two types of plumes: those formed by the burning item(s) in the fire room, and those formed by the jet of gases flowing through an opening. Thus, when the model calculates the flow of warm, lower layer gases through a low opening (e.g., the undercut of a "closed" door) by expansion of the smoke layer, they are assigned to the lower layer of the room into which they flowed. Thus, for a time the receiving room can show a lower layer temperature which exceeds that in the upper layer (a physically impossible condition). A better understanding of the flow within compartments in the context of a zone fire model would allow us to remove this anomaly. However, no hazard will exist during this time as the temperatures are low, and no gas species produced by the fire are carried through the opening until the upper layer drops to the height of the undercut.

Conversely, heat and gases are introduced into the lower layer of each room primarily due to heat transfer between the layer and compartment surfaces and mixing at connections between rooms Doorway mixing has been included in CFAST, assuming such mixing occurs as if the doorway flow were a normal fire plume. This may produce an underestimate of the lower layer concentrations. The most important manifestation of this

13

underestimate will be the temperature distribution between the upper and lower layers caused by radiation.

Tenability Limitations: Individual determinations are made for both incapacitation and lethality from temperature and toxicity, along with potential incapacitation from burns due to flux exposure. No interactions between temperature and toxicity are currently included (e.g., it is assumed but not known whether temperature exposure changes the rate of uptake of toxic species or increases the susceptibility to toxic species). The basis for the threshold values used and the derivation of the equations on which the toxicity calculation is based are provided in the Technical Reference volume in the chapter on Tenability Limits, which contains an extensive list of references. For all cases except flux exposure, the user can easily change the limit values used (and is encouraged to do so as a sensitivity test).

The limiting values of temperature exposure are based on the general literature, which includes some human data. The flux criterion comes from work done with pig skin, which is generally considered to be very similar to human skin. The toxicity data, however, are from the combustion toxicology literature which is based entirely on animal exposures (primarily rodents for lethality studies and nonhuman primates for incapacitation studies). The model assumes that humans will exhibit a similar physiological response.

A toxicity parameter, Ct (concentration multiplied by exposure time, often referred to as "exposure dose"), is used to indicate the toxic impact of the smoke without differentiating the constituent gases or the possibility of diminished oxygen. This is a broad assumption. Another toxicity parameter, the fractional exposure dose (FED), is also introduced. This represents the fraction of the lethal concentration that an individual has been exposed to over time. The FED parameter combines the effects and interactions of the gases CO, CO_2, and HCN along with the effect of diminished oxygen. The model on which the FED calculation is based, referred to as the N-Gas model [31].

1.3 What Is a Graphical User Interface (GUI)?

The FAST shell is a style of interface commonly referred to as a graphical user interface or GUI (pronounced GOO-EEE). Graphical refers to the use of lines, rectangles, colors, and shading to produce a three-dimensional interface appearance on a two-dimensional screen. A familiar GUI for many personal computer users is the MS-WINDOWS interface. The shell supports many of the features familiar to users of MS-WINDOWS applications but is not a MS-WINDOWS application. It is started from the DOS command line.

In order to provide a common base of familiarity, this section will discuss GUI concepts which are common between the application modules in FAST.

1.3.1 Using a Mouse or Other Pointing Device

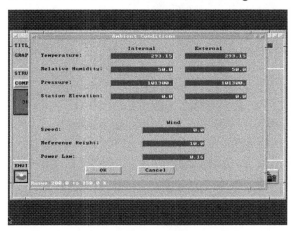

A pointing device such as a mouse or trackball is a hand held device frequently used in GUI applications to communicate selection information to the computer. For this guide, the term "mouse" will be used generically to indicate any appropriate pointing device. This guide references three types of mouse action. **Click** or **single-click** involves positioning the screen pointer on the item of interest and pressing and releasing the left mouse button once. **Double-click** involves positioning the screen pointer on the item of interest and pressing and releasing the left mouse button twice in rapid succession. A **drag** operation enables the user to move windows or items within windows to different positions on the screen. Dragging items involves positioning the screen pointer on the item of interest, pressing the left mouse button, moving the screen pointer to a new position while keeping the button depressed, then releasing the button when the item is positioned in the new location.

1.3.2 GUI Terminology

GUI interfaces are designed to assist the user in running multiple applications similar to an office worker having several project file folders open at one time. Using this parallel, the term **desktop** is used to refer to the full-screen background of a GUI application. A **window** is a rectangular, framed image drawn on the desktop and is used to view carefully selected portions of the larger application. Typically, the top frame, or **title bar**, of the window is used to provide a text title describing the purpose of that window. This clearly distinguishes one window on the desktop from other windows displayed at the same time.

When several windows are concurrently displayed, a problem could arise as to which window the user intends to apply keyboard entries. This issue is resolved in GUI applications through the concept of the **current** or **focus** window. The title bar display characteristics of the focus window are unique in comparison to all other currently displayed windows. The title bar of the focus window has a solid background while other windows have a shaded or color muted background.

In the top left corner of some windows, a horizontal bar is displayed inside a small square. Any window with this horizontal bar displayed can be removed from the screen, referred to as **closing the window**, by positioning the mouse pointer on this line and double-clicking.

Two types of windows are used within the FAST interface. The most common is referred to as a **dialog** or **modal window**. Modal windows are typically used for user input and can be identified by the row of buttons at the bottom of the window to allow the user to accept or reject the values shown in the window. The Ambient Conditions window, above, is an example of a modal window. When a modal window is displayed, the user cannot interact with the application through any other window or menu. The user must complete input for the current window or reject current input values in order to interact with other GUI windows or menus. Current input is accepted by clicking on the **OK** item. Current input values are rejected by clicking on the **Cancel** item or pressing the **Esc** key. Modal windows cannot be moved or sized.

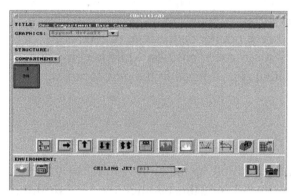

The **nonmodal window** or **overview window** is used as a background window in the GUI shell to summarize the current state of input. In FAST, the most frequently used nonmodal window is the fire scenario overview window. Nonmodal windows can be moved by the user. To move a nonmodal window, position the mouse pointer on the title bar and drag the window to a new position using the technique described in section 1.3.1. To make a nonmodal window the current or focus window, single-click on the title bar for that window.

The elements within GUI windows used to display information and request input from the user are referred to as **widgets**. Widgets within FAST have special display characteristics, responses, and associated functionality dependent on the widget type. Not all widgets support selection by the user. Refer to the detailed descriptions of each widget type in this section to determine selectability, functionality, and display characteristics. To move from one selectable widget to widgets below or to the right of the current widget, press the Tab key, or click on the desired widget using the mouse. To move to widgets above or to the left of the current widget, hold the Shift key down and press the Tab key, or click on the widget using the mouse. The following widgets are used at different times within the FAST interface:

Labels: Labels are used to prompt for the type of information requested in an associated edit widget. Labels are easily identified by the use of black text with no outline frame. Labels cannot be selected or modified by the user.

Edit widgets: Edit widgets are visually identified by white text displayed on a blue background. Edit widgets along with edit lists are the only widgets for which keyboard entry by the user is displayed to the screen. For integer and floating point edits, a message is displayed at the bottom of the window indicating the allowable range of input values for the current edit widget. If an entry is invalid, the range message is replaced with an error message displayed on a red background when the user attempts to select another widget. Corrections must be made to an invalid entry before the interface allows selection of another widget.

 **Text Buttons**: Text buttons are used to initiate user selected operations such as accepting or rejecting input or displaying additional windows for related input. The associated functionality is activated by a single mouse click on the button, or by pressing the Tab key until the screen pointer is positioned on the button then pressing Enter. Two special text buttons are available on most dialog windows. The *OK* button indicates to the application that entries in the edit widgets for this window are to be accepted and applied to the input specification. This acceptance pertains to the current use of the input editor, and does not affect the associated file stored on disk. To modify the disk file contents the user must save the input file following the procedure discussed in section 2.8.3. The *Cancel* button indicates to the application that entries in the edit widgets for this window are to be ignored, and the values which existed prior to use of this window are to be retained.

 Pull-down widgets: Pull-downs are used to provide the user with a complete list of all possible entries for a prompt field when the list is short and pre-determined by the application.

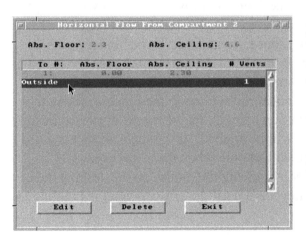 **Graphic icons**: Graphic icons use pictures to represent the functionality of a button. The associated functionality is activated by a single mouse click on the button, or by pressing the Tab key until the screen pointer is positioned on the button then pressing Enter.

Selection lists: Selection lists are used to provide a complete list of all possible options when that number potentially exceeds the size of a window. Only one entry may be selected from the list. The current entry selected is highlighted by a blue background with white text while the remaining available entries are indicated by a cyan background with white text. A selection is made by *double-clicking* with the mouse, by highlighting the desired selection with a single-click and pressing Enter, or by pressing the ↑ or ↓ keys to highlight the selection then pressing Enter.

Scroll bars: At times, the current window size is insufficient to display all available information, *e.g.*, a selection list contains more lines than are available for display on the screen. To accommodate the additional information, a vertical scroll bar is attached to the display window when the additional information is to be displayed in a top to bottom list. When the additional information is displayed in a left to right manner, a horizontal scroll bar is attached to the display window in order to access additional, previously undisplayed information. The displayed window performs a function similar to the use of a magnifying glass for viewing images on paper. Through the use of the appropriate direction arrows, the user is able to move the viewer up and down, or left and right, across the associated image. To view entries preceding, or above, the currently displayed entries in the window, press the up arrow icon (▣) on the vertical scroll bar. Press the down arrow icon (▣) to view entries below the currently displayed entries. If the horizontal scroll bar is available, press the left arrow icon (▣) or right arrow icon (▣) to pan the current viewer left or right across the associated image. Each time the user clicks on a direction arrow, the viewer scrolls one line or character in the corresponding direction. The rectangular box on the scroll bar indicates the current position within the full image to the user. To scroll the equivalent of one window in a direction, click on the appropriate scroll bar adjacent to the current position box in the direction scrolling is desired. If the user wishes to scroll down one window, click immediately below the current position box on the vertical scroll bar. To scroll right one window, click to the right of the current position box on the horizontal scroll bar.

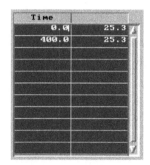

Edit lists: Edit lists are spreadsheets with display characteristics similar to the edit widgets. Background for each cell is blue with white text, and range messages are displayed at the bottom of the window. The range displayed is dependent on the context of the cell or block of the spreadsheet in which the text cursor is displayed. Range checks are activated in a manner similar to the edit widgets prohibiting the user from exiting a cell until the entry is valid. Movement between cells in an edit list requires pressing either the Shift-→ or Shift-← to move between columns from any position in a cell. Press the ↑ or ↓ to move between rows.

Cursors: Two types of cursors are used in a GUI interface. In addition to the blinking cursor (▣), or "I-beam," familiar to users of text-oriented interfaces, an **arrow pointer** (▣) is used to indicate the current mouse position. This becomes important when the user enters input or presses the Enter key from the keyboard since the widget responding to the input is *always* the focus widget. If the focus widget is an edit widget or an edit list, the I-beam is displayed inside the widget or cell to indicate where keyboard entry will be applied. If the focus widget is a text or graphics button, keyboard entry is applied to the widget only when the arrow pointer is displayed in that widget. A new focus widget is set by moving the mouse on the desktop then single-clicking, or by pressing the Tab key on the keyboard until the arrow pointer is pointing to the desired widget.

1.3.3 GUI shell menus

Menus provide lists of available applications or functions for selection by the user. Menus are displayed by clicking on the corresponding icon, or for some special menus, on a portion of the GUI screen. Once a menu is displayed, functions are selected by clicking on the item of interest with the mouse, or by pressing the ↑ or ↓ keys until the desired item is highlighted then pressing

Enter. The FAST GUI shell provides three main menus of interest: the **desktop menu**, the **file menu**, and the **toolbox menu**.

The **desktop menu** is used to select other modules within the FAST suite of applications. The name indicates that the desktop menu can be activated by clicking on the GUI desktop, the screen background. An alternate means for displaying the desktop menu involves selecting the desktop icon from the fire scenario overview window within the GUI shell. A summary of the applications associated with each of the desktop menu items is presented in section 1.5 below.

The **file menu** provides the user with a way to save input information in the currently selected file or in another filename specified by the user. Selection of the **save** option overwrites the current file while selection of the **save as** option prompts the user to specify a new filename. The file menu can be activated by clicking on the title bar of one of the fire scenario overview window within the GUI shell. An alternate means for displaying the file menu involves selecting the disk icon from the fire scenario overview window within the GUI shell.

The **toolbox menu** provides access to several quick calculation routines. Details of each routine are discussed in section 5 below. The toolbox menu can be activated by displaying the desktop menu then selecting the tools option. An alternate means for displaying the toolbox menu involves selecting the toolbox icon from the fire scenario overview window.

1.4 Starting FAST

To start FAST, change to the directory which contains the program and run it by changing to the directory where the software was installed and executing the program. The following commands are typical:

```
cd \FAST
FAST
```

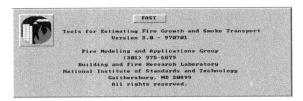

and are typed from the DOS command prompt (pressing the Enter key after each command). The FAST logo window is displayed. Press Enter to display the desktop menu from which other modules of the application suite can be selected. An overview of the FAST elements is presented in the next section. For detailed discussions, refer to the individual sections of this guide corresponding to desktop menu items of interest.

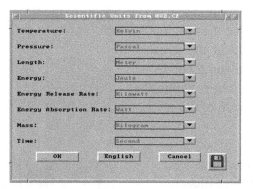

A window is automatically displayed the first time the program is executed to allow initial user selection of measurement units. Any combination of units may be used as desired. For the example cases in this manual, common metric units are used; units used for temperature, pressure, length, energy, energy release rate, energy absorption rate, mass and time are: Celsius, pascal, meter, joule, kilowatt, watt, kilogram and second.

To modify the settings for any  of the base measurements, click on the pull-down icon to the right of the measurement. A pull-down menu is displayed, listing the available measurement units. Select the display units desired by clicking on the corresponding menu entry. For example, temperature can be displayed in Kelvin, Celsius, Rankine, or Fahrenheit. Select *OK* to close the measurement units window. Measurement units may be changed at any time by selecting *Options* from the desktop menu, then selecting *User Specified Units* to display the measurement units window. For further details on customizing the units see section 6.2

1.5 Overview of FAST elements

FAST is composed of several interdependent modules which provide the different analyses desired by the individual user. The desktop menu discussed previously groups these modules according to the type of work and typical order in which a user might choose to execute the applications. This section provides a brief discussion of the applications and groupings with references to the appropriate section in this guide for detailed information.

File: Open / New: Specify details of the structure and fire scenario to be analyzed. For an example, refer to section 2. **Database:** View, modify, or select alternate databases for the thermal properties of compartment surfaces or additional burning objects.

Run: Run Fire Model: Calculate the fire and smoke characteristics for the details specified under input data. For details, refer to section 3. **Analyze Results**: Once calculations are completed, several options are available for interpreting and saving the results for further analysis.

Tools: Quick calculation tools which can be used to determine individual characteristics of the fire, *e.g.*, occurrence of flashover or mass flow through a vent. For details, refer to section 5.

Options: Customize the installed FAST suite of applications by specifying measurement display units, and licensing information. For details, refer to section 6.

Utilities: View, copy, and print files. For details, refer to section 6.

Help: Provides an overview of each graphic icon on the main FAST window and provides information on the version number and telephone support contacts for FAST.

2 Creating Input Data for FAST

FAST is an interactive, user-friendly program used to generate input data files for and run the CFAST model. As such, it is difficult to describe all the functions of the program in a reference guide. Rather, it is best learned through use. This section will describe the types of information entered on each of the windows of FAST. Users unfamiliar with the concepts of a Graphical User Interface (GUI) are encouraged to review these concepts in the Getting Started section of this guide before continuing with the Input Data section. Familiarity with GUI terminology and the use of a mouse is assumed throughout the remainder of this section.

2.1 Creating a New Input File – A Simple Example

To aid the first-time user in becoming familiar with the operation of FAST, this section provides a simple example of the use of FAST and includes detailed instructions of the use of the software for the example. For this example, we will simulate a fire in a two-room structure. Doors will connect the two rooms of the structure and connect the structure with the outdoors. The fire source will be a growing fire typical of combustibles found in single-family residences.

To start FAST, change to the directory which contains the program and run it by changing to the directory where the software was installed and executing the program. The following commands are typical:

```
cd \FAST
FAST
```

from the DOS command prompt (pressing the Enter key after each command). If the software was installed to a different directory, substitute an appropriate directory name for the cd \FAST commend above.

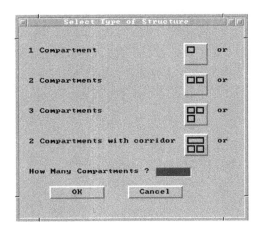

If this is the first time the program has been run since being installed, desired measurement units must be first selected. See section 1.4 for details on setting initial measurement units. After the FAST logo appears, the main desktop menu is displayed. Using the mouse, click on *File* then *New* to begin the definition of a new fire scenario. Initially, there are two steps to defining a new fire scenario to be modeled – selection of the geometry of the structure (the number of compartments and connections between the compartments) and a description of the fire.

23

Once *New* is selected, the structure selection window is displayed. From this window, the number of compartments and the arrangement of the compartments is defined. Once an initial selection has been made, the size of the compartments and any connections between compartments can be customized to fit the details of a specific scenario. For this example, choose the "2 Compartment" example by using the mouse to select the 2 compartment icon. Note that the selection highlights the icon with a bold black border. This selection defines two compartments 2.4 m wide by 3.6 m deep by 2.4 m high with doorways opening to the outdoors and connecting the compartments. Click on *OK* to accept the selection and close the window.

Following selection of the structure, the fire must be specified. For a wide range of fires, the fire growth can be accurately represented with a power law relation of the form

$$\dot{Q} \propto \alpha\ t^2 \tag{1}$$

where $\dot{Q}$ is the heat release rate of the fire, α is the fire intensity coefficient, and t is time [32]. A set of specific T-squared fires labeled slow, medium, and fast, with fire intensity coefficients (α) such that the fires reached 1055 kW (1000 BTU/s) in 600 s, 300 s, and 150 s, respectively were proposed for design of fire detection systems [33]. Later, these specific growth curves and a fourth called "Ultrafast" [34] which reaches 1055 kW in 75 s, gained favor in general fire protection applications.

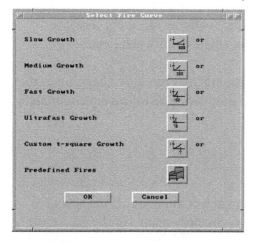

For this example, a medium T-squared growth rate fire will be specified. In a mixed collection of fuels selecting the medium curve is appropriate as long as there is no especially flammable item present. In a manner similar to the selection of the "2 Compartment" structure geometry above, select the medium growth rate fire by using the mouse to select the "Medium Growth" icon. Note that the selection highlights the icon with a bold black border. Click on *OK* to accept the selection and close the window. A new window is then displayed prompting for specific times to define the fire curve. For this example, the default values for the medium growth rate fire of 300 s and 900 s will be used. Click on *OK* to accept these defaults and close the window.

This completes the description of the example. Execution of the example case will continue in section 2.6. The next section describes the elements of FAST and provides a reference for all of the inputs to the software.

2.2 Details of Basic Fire Model Inputs

Once an input file has been created or opened, the fire scenario overview window is displayed. This window enables the user to see at a glance the major characteristics of the input file prior to running the model. It is possible to quickly determine the number of compartments (# of boxes drawn in structure section of window), the fire compartment (red box), and compartments with some type of sprinkler or detector (cyan or light blue boxes). Since the current CFAST model is concerned only with flow between compartments and not with the physical adjacencies of those compartments within the structure, no implications should be drawn from the adjacency of boxes displayed in this window to physical adjacencies of the corresponding structural compartments.

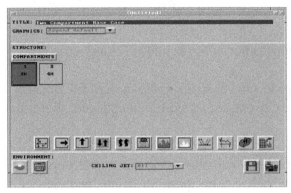

The fire scenario overview window is divided into three sections. The upper section provides the title for the input file. The second section pertains to the definition of compartments, flows between the compartments, placement of sprinkler/detectors, and the definition of fire curves. The final section of this overview window provides background information required to run the fire model such as the ambient conditions, filenames, and output times. Details for entering information into each of these sections are presented below.

In the first section of the overview window, each input file can be assigned a unique text description for identification purposes.

The structure overview or middle section of the window shows the number of compartments currently defined. For each compartment, text within the box indicates number of horizontal flow vents, *e.g.*, doors and windows (a number followed by H), and number of vertical flow vents, *e.g.*, vents in the ceiling or floor of the compartment (a number followed by V). The color of each compartment provides an indicator of the fire compartment (red), compartments which have detection/suppression devices (cyan), and/or compartments which contain other burning objects (yellow).

Prior to activating any of the graphics icons in the structure section of the overview window, a compartment must first be selected to determine how the activated icon will function. Click on compartment #1 of the input file, then press the geometry icon. Dimensions and surface materials for compartment #1 are displayed. Click on Cancel to close the geometry window, click on compartment #2 of the input file and press the geometry icon. The dimension and surface material details now reflect specifications for compartment #2. In a similar manner, experiment with the context changes in information displayed by pressing each of the graphics icons for different compartments. In the case of the time curve icon, the menu of possible curve definitions is dependent on the selected compartment along with other information provided for that compartment. If the compartment has a fire, the time curve icon allows entry of several different fire curves for that compartment. If the fire does not exist for the currently selected compartment, the time curve icon is grayed out and disabled. Each of the graphics icons in this middle section of the window can be matched to an icon image in section 2.8.2 in order to determine the related function and type of information requested.

The third section of the fire scenario overview window provides background information for the fire model run. Ambient conditions such as temperature and relative humidity are specified by pressing the ambient conditions icon. Length of simulation time along with print and spreadsheet files for the model run can be entered using the filenames icon.

Two final graphics icons are placed in the bottom right corner of the window. These icons are:

Write to file: save and save as. Select save to save changes to the current file or save as to save changes to a new file leaving the currently selected file unchanged. Refer to section 2.8.3.

Desktop: Provides access to the desktop menu which allows the user to select other modules within FAST; perform file utilities such as copy, print, or delete, and view files such as the current input file or the input editor error file generated when errors are found in opening an existing input file. Refer to section 1.5 for discussion of each of these modules.

2.2.1 Entering a Title for the Input File

TITLE: ▬▬▬▬▬▬▬▬▬▬▬▬▬▬ Before beginning to define the structure, it is typically best to start by assigning a title or description to the input file. The title is not used by the model, but is intended as an aid for the user in cataloguing the various fire scenario input files. Tab to the title field or move the mouse cursor to this field and click with the left mouse button. Enter the text desired. All titles maintain upper and lower case sensitivity as entered by the user.

2.2.2 Specifying Simulation Time and Spreadsheet Output

To specify the simulation time, display time, or output to spreadsheet file with output interval, Tab or move the mouse to the filename icon in the environment section of the fire scenario overview window, and click or press Enter.

Note the display of range and measurement units at the bottom of the window as each time edit widget is made the focus widget. To customize the units see section 6.2.

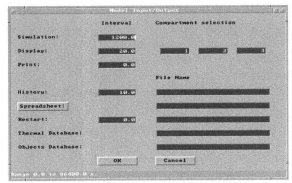

Simulation Interval: The length of time over which the simulation takes place. This is a required input which should be entered even if all other fields on the window are left unchanged. If the *File, New* option was used, a default value equal to the time the decay started plus the growth interval is provided.

Display Interval and Compartment Selection: The time interval between each graphical display of the output for runtime graphics. This output time pertains to the selection of the Graph button on the simulation status window and specifies how often the graph is updated. A default dependent upon the simulation time is provided. Up to three compartments may be selected to display in the simulation status window. Default values dependent on the number of compartments in the simulation are provided.

Print Interval: The time interval between printing of the output values. If omitted or less than or equal to zero, no printing of the output values will occur.

History Interval: The history file stores all of the output of the model at specified intervals in a format which can be evaluated using the *Analyze Results* option from the desktop menu. If a filename is entered, an output interval should also be entered.

Spreadsheet Interval and Filename: The spreadsheet file stores a subset of the output of the model at specified intervals in a comma-delimited alphanumeric format which can be read by most spreadsheet software. This is designed to be imported into a spreadsheet for further analysis or graphing of the results of the simulation. If a file name is entered, a default time interval dependent upon the simulation time is provided. Values to be output may be **Spreadsheet:** chosen by selecting the *Spreadsheet* text button..

Restart: These entries reference a previously generated CFAST history file and a time indicating an interval in the history file to use in restarting the fire model. Values consistent with those for this time in the previous run are obtained from the history file and provided to the model as initial values. The time entered must be an output entry in the previously created history file.

Thermal Database: Name of the thermal properties database used by the geometry window to select materials for different compartment surfaces. Care should be exercised when making such modifications.

Objects Database: Name of the objects database used by the other objects fire specification window to select the type of object and associated fire curve information. This should only be changed by the advanced user.

2.2.3 Setting Ambient Conditions

 To add or edit the internal and external ambient temperature, pressure, and station elevation along with information on external wind, Tab or move the mouse to the ambient conditions icon in the environment section of the fire scenario overview window, and click or press Enter.

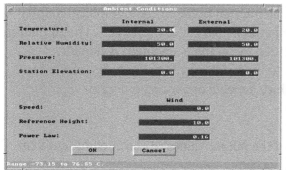

Note the display of range and measurement units at the bottom of the window as each edit widget is made the focus widget. To customize the units see section 6.2. Internal refers to conditions inside the structure while external indicates conditions outside the structure. Fields to be entered by the user along with default values are indicated below.

Internal Temperature: Initial temperature inside the structure. Default value 20 °C.

External Temperature: Initial temperature outside the structure. Default value 20 °C .

Relative Humidity: Initial relative humidity inside and outside the structure. Default values are 50 percent for the internal and external.

Pressure: Default values for inside and outside are standard atmospheric pressure at sea level, 101.3 kPa.

Station Elevation: The height where the pressure measurements were taken. This is the reference datum for calculating the density of the atmosphere as well as the temperature and pressure inside and outside of the structure as a function of height. Default value is 0, which is sea level.

Wind Speed, Scale Height, Power Law: The wind speed, scale height, and power law are used to calculate the wind coefficient for each vent connected to the outside. The wind velocity is specified at some reference height. The power law then provides a lapse rate for the wind speed. An assumption is that the wind speed is zero at the surface. The formula used to calculate the wind speed at the height of any vent is (wind speed) · ((vent height)/(scale height))$^{\text{(power law)}}$. The wind is applied to each external opening as a change in pressure outside of the vent.

2.2.4 Defining Compartments

 In order to model a fire scenario, the user must portray the geometry of the structure in terms of the size and elevation of every compartment in the structure. Thermophysical properties of the enclosing surfaces must also be specified by selecting surface materials in order to accurately model the transfer of heat through the surfaces. The maximum number of compartments is thirty. Connections between compartments are defined later in sections 2.2.5 and 2.2.6.

Two types of "add compartment" functionality are available. Compartments can be appended to the end of the currently displayed graphics list or inserted between existing compartments. If append is used, and two compartments currently exist, the new compartment would be compartment 3. If insert was selected with two compartments existing, and the current compartment is compartment 2, the new compartment would be numbered 2 and the current compartment would become 3. Compartments can be added to the structure by clicking on the compartment text button or by tabbing to the open area below the compartment button and pressing *INS* or *Ctrl-I* to insert, and *Ctrl-A* to append.

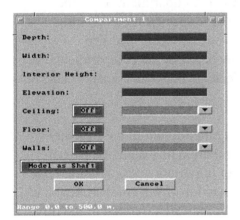 After selecting the type of add desired, the geometry window is displayed. Note the display of range and measurement units at the bottom of the window as each edit widget is made the focus widget. To customize the units see section 6.2.

Depth: Depth of the compartment as measured forward from the left, rear corner of the compartment.

Width: Width of the compartment as measured across from the left, rear corner of the compartment.

Interior Height: Height of the compartment.

Elevation: Height of the floor of the compartment with respect to the station elevation specified in the ambient condition window.

Ceiling, Floor, Walls: The *On/Off* button turns conduction for the associated surface on and off within this compartment. When the text "Off" is displayed on the button, the surface of the button is grayed out, or stippled. The adjacent text field for the thermal material is also stippled. The text field specifies the thermal material to use for conduction when the *On* button has been pressed. This material name can be entered by the user or selected from the database. To select a thermophysical material from the database, enter as much of the material database key word as is known, click on the pull-down icon, scroll the database until the desired material is viewed, and select by double-clicking, or highlight and press Enter. If the material key word is entered by the user, it must be a valid entry in the thermal properties database before the compartment can be generated.

 Model as Shaft: This determines how the compartment will be modeled whether as a rectilinear two zone volume or as a single zone. This option is off by default. If this option has been selected for a compartment, the modeling option is indicated by displaying * to the left of the compartment number in the fire scenario overview window.

Deleting Existing Compartments

To delete an existing compartment, select the compartment in the structure graphics list on the fire scenario overview window. Press *Alt-D* or the *Delete* key to delete the compartment.

2.2.5 Defining Connections for Horizontal Flow

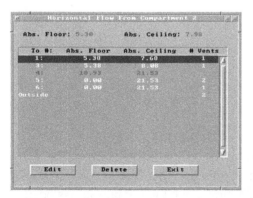 Horizontal flow connections may include doors between compartments or to the outdoors as well as windows in the compartments. These specifications do **not** necessarily correspond to physically connecting the walls between specified compartments. Rather, lack of an opening simply prevents flow between the compartments. Horizontal flow connections may also be used to account for leakage between compartments or to the outdoors.

To specify a horizontal flow opening, select the corresponding compartment in the structure graphics list on the fire scenario overview window. The determination of which of a pair of compartments should be selected as the first compartment is not important since defining flow connections from compartment 1 to 2 immediately implies connections from compartment 2 to 1. Flow connections do not indicate direction of the flow, but simply enable the flow to occur. Direction of flow is determined by the characteristics of the physical phenomena such as pressure and temperature at the time the model is run. The true significance of selection of a from compartment is reflected in the positioning of the connection. Once a compartment has been selected as the from compartment, it will become the reference compartment for specification of the position of the connection. Tab or move the mouse to the horizontal flow icon, and click or press Enter.

All compartments with currently defined elevation and height of compartment are displayed in the selection list. Horizontal connections can only be created between compartments that

physically overlap in elevation at some point. Those compartments for which such a connection is possible are highlighted in white in the selection list. Compartments which cannot be connected because of this physical constraint have been grayed out. To complete the connection, click on the compartment in the selection list to which flow is desired and press the Edit button, or double-click on the selection with the mouse.

Note the display of range and measurement units at the bottom of the window as each cell in the edit list widget is made the focus widget. To customize the units see section 6.2.

It is possible to define a total of four (4) horizontal flow connections between any pair of compartments using the spreadsheet. In order to complete each flow definition, the size and location of the connection with respect to the floor of the compartment must be entered. There is no provision for the specification of the placement of a vent along the length of the wall. Vent numbers are automatically defined when the file is saved in order to uniquely identify each of the connection pairs. The vent number assigned corresponds to the row of the spreadsheet in which the entries are made. The user is free to enter vent information on any of the four rows provided. To move to a cell either click on that cell using the mouse, or use Shift-→ and Shift-← to move right and left, and ↑ and ↓ to change rows.

Width: The width of the opening.

Soffit: Position of the top of the opening above the floor of the compartment selected as the first compartment from the graphics list. This compartment is displayed as the from compartment on this window with corresponding elevation and height.

Sill: Sill height is the height of the bottom of the opening above the floor of the compartment selected as the first compartment from the graphics list. This compartment is displayed as the from compartment on this window with corresponding elevation and height.

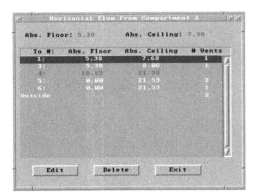

Wind: The wind coefficient is the cosine of the angle between the wind vector and the vent opening. This applies only to vents which connect to the outside. The range of values is -1.0 to 1.0 with a default value of zero.

Deleting existing connections: To delete all existing connections between a pair of compartments, from the selection list, highlight the compartment to which all connections are to be deleted, and press the Delete

31

button. To delete individual connections between a pair of compartments, select the compartment to which the connection is to be deleted, and press the Edit button. Move to the spreadsheet row representing the vent to be deleted, and press Alt-d to delete the entry or Alt-e to erase the entry. Deleting the entry will move all entries below the current row up one row resulting in a renumbering of remaining vents. Erasing the entry will leave all other rows in current positions and will retain current vent number assignments.

2.2.6 Defining Connections for Vertical Flow

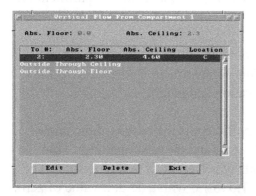 Vertical flow connections include any vertical flow openings, such as holes between compartments or to the outdoors. These specifications do **not** correspond to physically connecting the ceiling and floor between specified compartments. Lack of an opening prevents flow. Vertical flow connections may also be used to account for leakage between compartments or to the outdoors. Opening and closing of these connections is not handled by the fire model at this time – vents are fully open if specified in the data file.

Vertical flow connections are specified by selecting one compartment as the current compartment in the structure graphics list on the fire scenario overview window. The determination of which of a pair of compartments should be selected as the first compartment is not important since defining flow connections from compartment 1 to 2 immediately implies connections from compartment 2 to 1. Flow connections do not indicate direction of the flow, but simply enable the flow to occur. Direction of flow is determined by the characteristics of the physical phenomena such as pressure and temperature at the time the model is run. The significance of selection of first compartment is reflected in the specification of the position of the connection. Once a compartment has been selected as the first compartment, it will become the reference compartment for positioning of the connection.

Tab or move the mouse to the vertical flow icon, and click or press Enter. All compartments with currently defined elevation and height of compartment are displayed in a selection list. Vertical connections can only be created between compartments that could be physically stacked based on specified floor and ceiling elevations for the compartments. Some overlap between the absolute floor height of one compartment and the absolute ceiling height of another compartment is allowed. However, whether the compartments are stacked or overlap somewhat, the ceiling/floor absolute elevations must be within 0.01 m of each other. Those compartments for which such a connection is possible are highlighted in white in the selection list. Compartments which cannot be connected because of this physical constraint have been grayed out.   To complete the connection, click on the compartment to which flow is desired and press the Edit button, or double-click on the selection with the mouse.

32

Note the display of range and measurement units at the bottom of the window as each edit widget is made the focus widget. To customize the units see section 6.2.

It is possible to define only one vertical flow connection between any pair of internal compartments. However, two connections may be specified from a compartment to the outdoors, one through the ceiling and the other through the floor. In order to complete each definition, the shape and area of the opening must be entered. Once a shape has been selected, the maximum possible area for a vent with that shape is calculated by the input editor. This value will be the upper bound allowed for the area of the opening. There is no provision for the specification of the placement of the vent along the width or breadth of the ceiling. The position of the vent in the floor or ceiling of a compartment is automatically calculated by the input editor based upon the specified elevations for the pair of compartments.

Shape: Circle or square.

Area: The effective area of the opening. For a hole, it would be the actual opening. For a diffuser, the effective area is somewhat less than the geometrical size of the opening.

Deleting existing connections: To delete an existing connection between a pair of compartments, from the selection list, highlight the compartment to which the connection is to be deleted, and press the Delete button.

2.2.7 Adding Sprinklers and Detectors

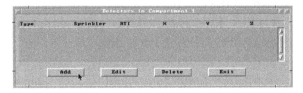

Sprinklers and detectors are both considered detection devices by the FAST model and are handled using the same input window. Detection is based upon heat transfer to the detector. Fire suppression by a user-specified water spray begins once the associated detection device is activated. A maximum of 20 sprinklers or detectors can be included for any input file and model run. These can be in one compartment or scattered throughout the structure. Sprinklers and detectors are added by selecting the compartment into which the device is to be placed from the structure graphics list in the fire scenario overview window. Tab or move the mouse to the sprinkler icon, and click or press Enter.

To change the specification for an existing sprinkler or detector, highlight the entry and press the Edit button, or double-click with the mouse. To add a new sprinkler or detector, press the Add button.

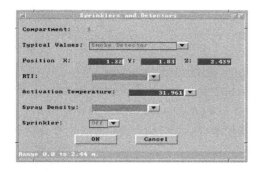

Note the display of range and measurement units at the bottom of the window as each edit widget is made the focus widget. To customize the units see section 6.2.

In order to complete the definition, the type of detection device, position of the detector within the compartment, and the type of sprinkler must be specified. If the sprinkler is turned on, the detection device is considered a sprinkler. For sprinklers, the response time index (RTI), activation temperature, and spray density must also be entered. Default values are provided for residential and commercial sprinklers.

Typical Values: Several sets of default values for typical detection / suppres-sion devices can be chosen. The choice of smoke detector, heat detector, residential sprinkler, or commercial sprinkler effects the default RTI, activation temperature, and sprinkler characteristics below. By default, the device is placed in the center of the compartment at ceiling level.

X Position: Position of the device as a distance from the rear wall of the compartment. See diagram.

Y Position: Position of the device as a distance from the left wall of the compartment. See diagram.

Z Position: Height of the device above the floor of the compartment. See diagram.

z = HR

DR = Depth
BR = Width
HR = Height

(0,0,0)

y = BR

Center = (DR/2, BR/2,0)

x = DR

RTI: The RTI (Response Time Index) quantifies how rapidly the detector link temperature rises in response to immersion in a hot ceiling jet. For residential sprinklers, a default RTI of 50 $(m \cdot s)^{\frac{1}{2}}$ is assumed. For commercial sprinklers, a default RTI of 100 $(m \cdot s)^{\frac{1}{2}}$ is assumed. RTI is ignored for smoke detectors. Values for typical devices, chosen from NFPA 13 [35], can be selected with the pull-down list (⬛) to the right of the *RTI* edit widget. These typical values are representative of often-used designs and are converted into appropriate units for input to the model calculation and entered directly into the *RTI* edit widget.

Activation Temperature: The temperature at or above which the detector link activates. For residential sprinklers, an activation temperature of 57 °C (135 °F) is assumed. For commercial sprinklers, an activation temperature of 74 °C (165 °F) is assumed. Smoke detectors are simulated by an activation temperature of 11 °C above ambient. Values for typical devices can be selected with the pull-down list (⬛) to the right of the *Activation Temperature* edit widget. These typical values are representative of often-used designs and are converted into appropriate units for input to the model calculation and entered directly into the *Activation Temperature* edit widget.

Spray Density: The amount of water dispersed by a water spray-sprinkler. The units for spray density are length/time. These units are derived by dividing the volumetric rate of water flow by the area protected by the water spray. The spray density may be measured by collecting water in a pan located within the spray area and recording the rate-of-rise in the water level. Values for typical devices, chosen from NFPA 13, can be selected with the pull-down list (☷) to the right of the *Spray Density* edit widget. These typical values are representative of often-used designs and are converted into appropriate units for input to the model calculation and entered directly into the *Spray Density* edit widget.

Sprinkler: If turned off, the device is handled as a heat or smoke detector only – values entered for RTI, trigger value, and spray density are ignored. The suppression calculation is based upon an experimental correlation by Evans [36], and depends upon the RTI, trigger value, and spray density to determine the behavior of the sprinkler. Several cautions should be observed when using estimates of sprinkler suppression within the model: 1) the first sprinkler activated controls the effect of the sprinkler on the heat release rate of the fire. Subsequent sprinklers which may activate have no additional effect on the fire simulation. 2) The fire suppression algorithm assumes the effect of the sprinkler is solely to reduce the heat release rate of the fire. Any effects of the sprinkler spray on gas temperatures or mixing within the compartment are ignored. 3) The sprinkler always reduces the heat release rate of the fire. The ability of a fire to overwhelm an underdesigned sprinkler is not modeled. 4) Since the dynamics of the sprinkler and direct effects of the spray on gas temperatures and velocities are not modeled, calculated times of activation of secondary sprinklers and / or detectors after the first sprinkler is activated should be ignored.

2.2.8 Defining the Main Fire

The main fire is typically the first fire to ignite and the source of ignition for additional fires. To define the main fire, the compartment of fire origin must be selected and chemical properties entered. Time-dependent combustion properties are entered in section 2.2.9 below. Only a single fire source can be specified here. Additional fires are specified in section 2.3.7.

To position the fire in a compartment, select that compartment as the current compartment in the structure graphics list in the fire scenario overview window. Tab or move the mouse to the fire icon, and click or press Enter. Note the display of range and measurement units at the bottom of the window as each edit widget is made the focus widget. To customize the units see section 6.2.

Type: Unconstrained, constrained, or constrained with flashover. The burning rate for a constrained fire is limited by the available oxygen entrained into the plume. The default is

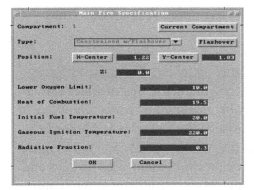

constrained with flashover. If an unconstrained type is selected, only the toxic combustion products can be specified for species. All other species curves are available for a constrained fire type. If constrained with flashover is selected, an additional button is available to defined the post-flashover burning characteristics. To turn the fire off, but retain any associated fire characteristics for future use, select *OFF*.

X Position: Position of the fire as a distance from the rear wall of the compartment. See diagram.

Y Position: Position of the fire as a distance from the left wall of the compartment. See diagram.

Z Position: Height of the fire above the floor. See diagram.

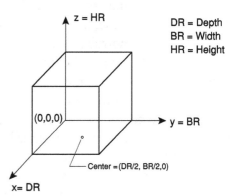

Lower Oxygen Limit: The limit on the ratio of oxygen to other gases in the system below which a flame will not burn. This is applicable only to constrained fires. The default value is 10. This limit applies to the overall system, not to the individual combustion regions.

Heat of Combustion: Heat of combustion of the fuel. A default value for wood of 19.5 MJ/kg is assumed. Any value entered directly for the heat of combustion is considered a constant value throughout the simulation. If a constant value is desired, fire specification is completed by entering either the pyrolysis rate or the heat release rate curve in section 2.2.9. The remaining undefined variable, pyrolysis rate or heat release rate, is then automatically calculated. If time dependent values are available for the mass loss rate and rate of heat release, enter these values in section 2.2.9 and the model will calculate the corresponding time history for the heat of combustion.

Initial Fuel Temperature: Typically, the initial fuel temperature is the same as the ambient temperature specified on the ambient conditions window. This may not be true if significant conductive or radiative heat transfer affects the fuel.

Gaseous Ignition Temperature: Minimum temperature for ignition of the fuel as it flows from a compartment through a vent into another compartment. If omitted, the default is arbitrarily set to the initial fuel temperature plus 200 °C.

Radiative Fraction: The fraction of heat released by the fire that goes into radiation. A default value of 0.3 is assumed [37]. For other fuels, the work or Tewarson [38], McCaffrey [39], or

Koseki [40] is available for reference. These place the typical range for the radiative fraction from about 0.15 to 0.5.

Additionally, the fire specification window has several buttons which serve purposes unique to this window.

Current Compartment button allows the user to select from the structure graphics list a compartment which previously did not contain the fire, click on the fire icon, press the *Current Compartment* button, and the fire is relocated to that compartment. All specifications for the fire remain unchanged except for the fire location. The fire position is recalculated so that the **relative** position in the original compartment is maintained in the new compartment.

X-Center button allows the X position to be automatically calculated using previously specified dimensions for the compartment. Pressing this button indicates to the model that the fire should remain in the center of the X position regardless of changes to the compartment dimensions or relocation of the fire to other compartments. Once the user manually enters the corresponding X Position field, however, the X center functionality is terminated.

Y-Center button allows the Y position to be automatically calculated using previously specified dimensions for the compartment. Pressing this button indicates to the model that the fire should remain in the center of the Y position regardless of changes to the compartment dimensions or relocation of the fire to other compartments. Once the user manually enters the corresponding Y Position field, however, the Y center functionality is terminated.

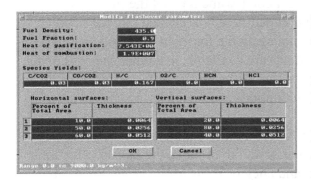

Flashover: Clicking the *Flashover* button displays the flashover screen. The flashover screen has a number for entries of information needed to continue the simulation in flashover. Default values are provided for all fields.

Fuel density: Average density of the fuel burning during post-flashover burning

Fuel fraction: the fraction of the total material that will pyrolyze and lead to combustion.

Heat of gasification: the amount of energy necessary to pyrolyze a unit mass of the fuel – that is turn it from a solid to a gas.

Heat of combustion: the amount of energy a given mass of the fuel gives off when it burns.

Combustion chemistry: The next row of entries defines the combustion chemistry for the fuel. *C/CO2* field is the ratio of mass of carbon produced for smoke to the mass of carbon dioxide produced in combustion of the fuel. *CO/CO2* is the ratio of mass of CO produced to the mass of

CO2 produced in combustion of the fuel. *H/C* is the ratio of the mass of hydrogen to carbon in the fuel. *O2/C* is the mass of oxygen liberated to the atmosphere by pyrolization to the mass of carbon in the fuel. *HCN* and *HCl* are the ratio of the mass of HCN and HCl produced to the mass of CO2 in combustion.

Available fuel: These tables are used to put in the amount of fuel available in the room. One table is for fuel with its surface oriented horizontally; the other is for fuel with its surface oriented vertically. For each orientation, up to three thicknesses of fuel can be specified. The amount of fuel is given as a percentage of the total room surface with the same orientation. For example, for horizontal fuel, this is the percentage of the total wall surface area. The area in a table can add up to more than 100 percent to allow for the inclusion of surface area of furniture, partitions, or other material in the compartment. When all the inputs are satisfactory clicking on the *OK* button continues the run.

2.2.9 Specifying Time-Dependent Fire Curves

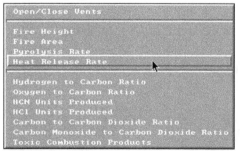 Two types of time-dependent curves are available for use with the fire model. The first specify the open and close characteristics of horizontal flow openings such as windows or doors. The second relates specifically to the main fire and is used to specify the combustion characteristics of the fire.

To define a time-dependent curve, a compartment must be selected from the structure graphics list in the fire scenario overview window. If the current compartment is not the fire compartment, indicated by part or all of the current compartment box painted red, time curves specifying combustion characteristics of the fire are not available for input. If an unconstrained fire type is specified, only the toxic combustion products are available. No other species curves may be specified for the unconstrained fire type. If neither the main fire nor horizontal openings exist for the current compartment, no time curve input options are available.

Specifying Time-Dependent Combustion Properties: Select the fire compartment from the structure graphics list in the fire scenario overview window. Tab or move the mouse to the time curve icon, and click or press Enter. Select the desired curve, *e.g., Heat Release Rate*, from the menu.

Note the display of range and measurement units at the bottom of the window as each cell in the edit list widget is made the focus widget. To customize the units see section 6.2. If no other time-dependent curves have been entered previously for this input file, no entries will be displayed in the spreadsheet. To enter time curves for the first time, Tab to the spreadsheet or click on the first cell using the mouse. Enter the actual time at which each fire property is

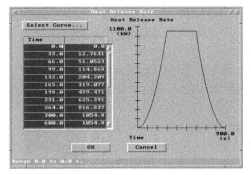

evaluated. Use the vertical scroll bar to enter additional entries beyond those initially displayed. Refer to the GUI Terminology section 1.3.2 of this reference guide for an explanation of the use of scroll bars in the GUI interface.

Movement between time cells is handled using the ↑ and ↓ keys. To insert a new time entry between two existing rows, press *Alt-I*. To delete a row, press *Alt-D*. Deleting a row moves all rows following the deleted row up one row. If the entry is to be erased, but all other rows are to remain in current positions, press *Alt-E* to erase the row. Time entry value ranges are constrained by the entries in surrounding time cells so that time entries within a column of the spreadsheet are ever increasing values. The maximum value allowed is 86 400 seconds. Once time entries have been completed for one curve, these time points are available for all other curves. Consequently, only the abscissa values will need to be entered for subsequent curves.

Once the time points have been specified in the first column of the curve spreadsheet, select the top cell of the right column to begin entering the combustion property curve. Keyboard movement from the left column to the right column can be handled by pressing Shift-→ and then the ↑ key until the first cell is reached. Specify the values for the combustion property according to details discussed below. As values are entered in the right column, the fire curve corresponding to time and abscissa entries is plotted on the graph to the right of the spreadsheet.

Fire Height: The height of the base of the flames above the floor of the compartment of fire origin. The values entered are added to the z-position value entered for the main fire in order to determine the exact fire height. This provides the user with the ability to define an appropriate shape for the fire height curve, and then adjust the actual height by changing only one entry, the z position, as opposed to modifying all entries in the curve. The key word affected by input of this curve is FHIGH.

Fire Area: The area of the fire at the base of the flames.

Pyrolysis Rate: The rate at which fuel is pyrolyzed at times corresponding to each point of the specified fire. Note concerns below regarding the over specification of the fire curves.

Heat Release Rate: The heat release rate of the specified fire. Note concerns below regarding the over specification of the fire curves.

Over specifying Fire Curves: Since the heat of combustion, heat release rate, and pyrolysis rate are related properties, the fire curve can be over specified. If each of the three parameters, heat of combustion from the fire specification window, heat release rate curve, and pyrolysis rate have been specified, the fire is over specified. The input editor accounts for this by using the two most

39

recently entered to calculate the third parameter. This allows for two typical scenarios depending on whether the user desires to use a constant value heat of combustion or a heat of combustion curve. If the user desires to use a constant value heat of combustion, this value should first be entered in the fire specification window. Either the pyrolysis rate or heat release rate curve is then entered. If the pyrolysis rate curve is entered, the heat release rate is automatically calculated by multiplying each entry in the pyrolysis rate curve by the constant value heat of combustion. If the heat release rate is entered, the pyrolysis rate curve is calculated by dividing each entry of the heat release rate curve by the constant value heat of combustion. For the user desiring a heat of combustion curve rather than a constant value, the user should enter the heat release rate and pyrolysis rate curves separately. The model will calculate the appropriate heat of combustion curve prior to execution. One caution regarding this approach. If a user desiring a constant value heat of combustion saves the input file and returns later, the input editor views the heat release rate and pyrolysis rate curves as the last two properties entered. If the user then makes modifications to entries in one of the curves, the other curve will not be automatically calculated. The user must make a change to the heat of combustion in order to get the second curve recalculated.

Hydrogen to Carbon Ratio: The mass ratio of hydrogen to carbon as it becomes available from the fuel. Units are kg/kg. The key word affected by input of this curve is HCR.

Oxygen to Carbon Ratio: The mass ratio of oxygen to carbon as it becomes available from the fuel. Units are kg/kg. The key word affected by input of this curve is O2.

HCN Units Produced: Kilogram of hydrogen cyanide produced per kilogram of fuel pyrolized. The key word affected by input of this curve is HCN.

HCL Units Produced: Kilogram of hydrogen chloride produced per kilogram of fuel pyrolized. The key word affected by input of this curve is HCL.

Soot to Carbon Dioxide Ratio: Ratio of the mass of carbon to carbon dioxide produced by the oxidation of the fuel. This curve is used to simulate soot production. The key word affected by input of this curve is OD. The assumption is that most of the mass of a soot particle is from the carbon atoms.

Carbon Monoxide to Carbon Dioxide Ratio: Ratio of the mass of carbon monoxide to carbon dioxide produced by the oxidation of the fuel. The key word affected by input of this curve is CO.

Toxic Combustion Products: Kilogram of "toxic" combustion products produced per kilogram of fuel pyrolized. The key word affected by input of this curve is CT.

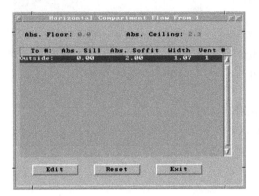

It is recommended that all other fire related curves be entered prior to entering the open/close opening characteristics. This is intended to assist the user. Once a time line has been entered using the fire combustion properties curves, a time line of default values is generated for each of the horizontal openings in the structure. These default values set each opening fully open. It is then only necessary for the user to modify those entries for which the opening is not fully open. If the default value of fully open is desired for all horizontal openings defined, no further entry is necessary.

Once a compartment has been selected from the structure graphics list in the fire scenario overview window, click on the time-dependent curve icon. For a compartment with horizontal flow openings, clicking on the time-dependent curve icon displays a selection list window. This display is similar to the one used when selecting compartment connections, but is now limited to those compartments for which horizontal connections were previously specified. All openings

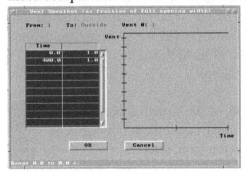

defined between each pair of rooms are enumerated and uniquely identified by an internally assigned integer. Remember that the vent numbering is determined by the row of the spreadsheet used when defining the horizontal flow opening. Select the vent for which open/close characteristics are to be specified by selecting the compartment and appropriate vent number entry from the selection list. Double-click on the entry, or click on the *Edit* button.

In the right column of the spreadsheet, modify those entries for which the opening is not fully open using a fraction. A value of 1.0 represents a fully open vent. A value of 0.5 would specify an opening which was halfway open.

2.2.10 Tools

Quick estimation tools are available through the input editor to calculate values such as flashover conditions or mass flow through a vent or to provide estimates for input parameters for FAST simulations. Select the compartment to be modeled from the structure graphics list in the fire scenario overview window. Tab or move the mouse to the tools icon, and click or press Enter. The FIREFORM menu is displayed.

Select the desired estimation tool by clicking on that entry in the displayed menu. An input window for the selected estimation routine is displayed.

Default values based on previously entered specifications for the selected compartment and fire scenario are provided for each appropriate edit widget. Make the appropriate modifications for default values and enter all values for which no default is provided. Refer to the appropriate subsections of section 5 below for additional details for each estimation calculation.

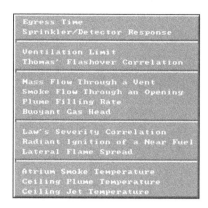

2.3 Details of Advanced Fire Model Inputs

2.3.1 Building HVAC Systems

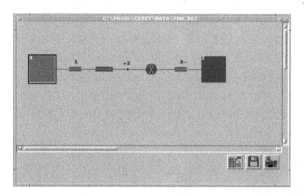

For input files detailing mechanical ventilation system specifications, a second type of overview window is available. The mechanical ventilation overview window provides a graphical, network representation of the defined mechanical ventilation system.

Compartments of the structure correspond to the blue compartment icon, fans correspond to fan icon, ducts are represented by the duct icon ▄▄▄ , compartment ventilation openings correspond to the vent icon ▇▇▇ , and fittings between ducts and fans correspond to the fitting icon ━╋━ . If the main fire compartment is included in the mechanical ventilation system, the corresponding icon is the red compartment icon. The HVAC overview window provides a means for the user to draw a network representation of the system to be modeled. The network can be scrolled left to right as well as top to bottom in the window using the corresponding directional scroll bars.

Creating a new mechanical ventilation system

Mechanical ventilation systems are created by first selecting from the structure graphics list the compartment to be connected to the HVAC system through a diffuser or vent. Tab or move the mouse to the mechanical ventilation icon, and click or press Enter. The HVAC

42

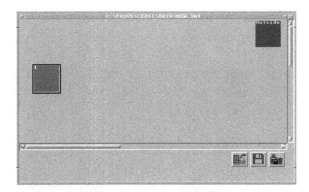

overview window is displayed with a square graphics icon representing the selected compartment and an additional square icon representing the outdoors.

To build a branch of the mechanical ventilation system, click on the compartment icon on the HVAC overview window which corresponds to the previously selected compartment.

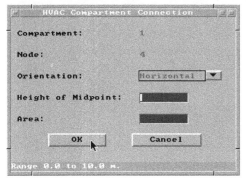

The vent connection window is displayed.

Enter the vent connection details according to the discussion in section 2.3.2 below. Once the vent connection details are accepted by pressing the *OK* button, a blinking vent icon is displayed on the HVAC overview window.

Position the icon to the desired location by moving the mouse cursor. Once the icon is properly positioned, click once with the mouse.

Continue building the HVAC branch by clicking on the vent icon. A selection menu is displayed. Select either a duct ▬▬ or fan ⊗ from the displayed menu. The user is prompted in the lower portion of the window to position the open end of the branch for the new component within the HVAC overview window. To position the open end, move the mouse to the desired position in the window, and click once with the mouse. A detail window corresponding to the HVAC component selected by the user from the previous component menu is displayed.

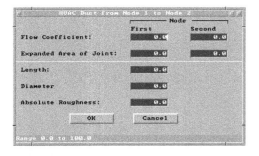

Refer to the appropriate sections 2.3.5 and 2.3.4 below for fan or duct input requirements depending on previous menu selection. Once the HVAC component input specifications are completed and accepted, the detail window for the open fitting is displayed.

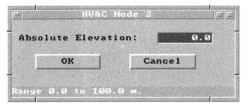

The absolute height of the fitting must be specified. Once input for the fitting is accepted, the graphics icon for the new component is displayed in the HVAC overview window along with a small dot representing the open end of the branch.

43

The branch can be continued from the disconnected dot icon. As the system is created, new branches can be started at any of the dot icons previously displayed.

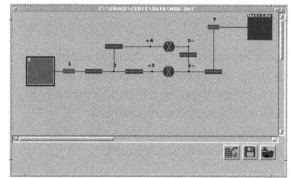

Additional branches cannot be generated from the vent ▬ icons which always connect ducts or fans directly to a compartment.

Continue building branches of the HVAC system from dot icons until the end of a branch, another compartment, or the outdoors is reached. If the branch terminating compartment is not currently displayed on the HVAC overview window, click on the structure icon The structure overview window is displayed. Select the compartment to which to connect the end of the branch by clicking on the compartment in the structure graphics list, then return to the HVAC overview window by clicking on the HVAC icon.

The selected compartment icon is now available on the HVAC overview window. Position the mouse cursor on the open fitting for the last specified branch indicated by an unconnected dot icon. Drag the dot icon until it overlaps the compartment icon corresponding to the terminating structure compartment, or outdoors.

The graphics dot icon changes appearance from an internal fitting to a vent. Double-click on the new vent icon to complete the remaining vent characteristics.

Continue building branches to the system in a similar manner. All graphics icon representations can be dragged on the HVAC overview window and positioned as the user desires. The vertical and horizontal scroll bars can be used to allow the user to extend systems to the right and bottom of the currently displayed window. Input for each piece in the mechanical ventilation system is described in more detail below.

Editing an existing HVAC system component

To edit an existing system and modify the characteristics of either a vent, duct, fan, or internal fitting, double-click on the corresponding graphics icon and enter details according to the appropriate section below.

Deleting an existing HVAC system component

To delete existing connections within a branch, click on the duct or fan to be deleted, and press the Delete key. The selected icon is deleted from the overview window, and two dot icons representing the open fittings remain. Create a new fan or duct from either of the dot icons in a manner similar to that discussed previously in *Creating a new mechanical ventilation system*. If no fan or duct is to replace the deleted fan or duct, merge the open fittings by positioning the mouse over one dot icon, then drag until it overlaps the remaining dot icon.

To delete compartment connections, click on the vent to be deleted, and press the Delete key. If the selected icon is part of an existing mechanical ventilation branch, the icon is replaced by an unconnected dot icon. Build additional components from this icon according to specifications in *Creating a new mechanical ventilation system*, or connect to another compartment by dragging the dot icon until it overlaps the desired compartment icon. If the selected icon is not connected to a branch of the mechanical ventilation system, it is deleted.

All compartment icons on the HVAC overview window can be deleted except for the icon corresponding to the outdoors. Delete compartment icons by highlighting the icon and pressing alt-d or the Delete key. If an internal fitting icon remains on the screen with no connected ducts or fans, it can be deleted by highlighting and pressing alt-d or the Delete key.

Merging HCAC system branches

Fittings within branches can be merged by dragging one dot icon until it overlaps another existing icon. Internal fittings cannot be merged with existing compartment vent connections. Two dot icons representing HVAC system fittings cannot be merged together if those fittings are the defining end points of an existing fan or duct component.

Inserting new components

To insert new HVAC system components between two existing fittings, click on the dot icon or compartment vent representing one of the fittings, select the type of component from the displayed menu, and click on the terminating dot icon in response to the positioning message. Specification is completed by entering details in the corresponding detail window as discussed in sections 2.3.5 and 2.3.4 below. New components cannot be added between two fittings if those fittings are the defining end points of an existing fan or duct component.

2.3.2 HVAC Vent or Diffuser

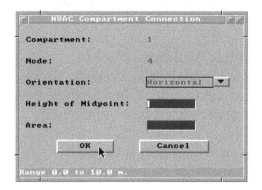

To edit an existing vent, double-click on the corresponding graphics icon ▬▬ on the HVAC overview window. The HVAC vent window is displayed

Note the display of range and measurement units at the bottom of the window as each edit widget is made the focus widget. To customize the units see section 6.2. The MVOPN key word in the input file is affected by changes using this icon.

45

Orientation: The orientation of the diffuser relative to the floor of the compartment. A horizontal diffuser implies vertical flow through the ceiling or floor of the compartment. A vertical diffuser implies horizontal flow through a wall of the compartment.

Height of the Midpoint: Height of the duct opening above the floor of the compartment measured from the midpoint of the register.

Area: Cross-sectional area of the opening into the compartment.

2.3.3 HVAC Internal Connection or Fitting

To edit an existing internal fitting, double-click on the corresponding graphics icon on the HVAC overview window. An edit window is displayed

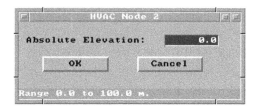

Note the display of range and measurement units at the bottom of the window as each edit widget is made the focus widget. To customize the units see section 6.2. The INELV key word in the input file is affected by changes using this icon.

Absolute height: Height of this fitting with respect to the reference elevation entered on the Ambient Conditions window.

2.3.4 HVAC Duct

To edit an existing HVAC duct, double-click on the corresponding graphics icon ~~~~ on the HVAC overview window. The edit window is displayed.

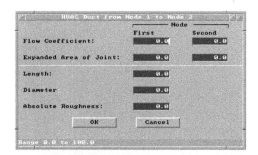

Note the display of range and measurement units at the bottom of the window as each edit widget is made the focus widget. To customize the units see section 6.2. The MVDCT key word in the input file is affected by changes using this icon.

Flow Coefficients: These coefficients allow for expansion or contraction at the ends of the duct. To use a straight through connection with no expansion or contraction, set to zero. Values for these flow coefficients have been tabulated for a substantial number of connection geometries [41], [42].

Expanded Area of Joint: The representative cross-sectional area of the duct at the ends.

Length: Length of the duct.

Diameter: All duct work is assumed to be circular. Other shapes must use an equivalent diameter (see, for example, [43], [44]):

$$A_{equivalent} = \frac{A_{duct}}{Perimeter_{wetted}}$$

Absolute Roughness: The absolute roughness affects laminar flow friction losses within the duct. It is obtained from reference books and undergraduate texts on fluid flow [41].

2.3.5 HVAC Fan

To edit an existing HVAC fan, double-click on the corresponding graphics icon 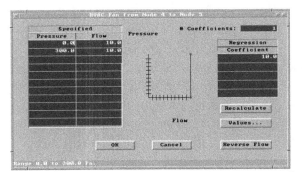 on the HVAC overview window. The edit window is displayed.

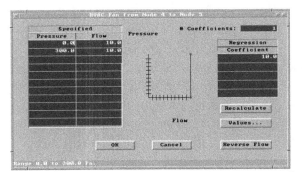

Note the display of range and measurement units at the bottom of the window as each edit widget is made the focus widget. To customize the units see section 6.2. The MVFAN key word in the input file is affected by changes using this icon.

Specified Curve: User specified values for flow versus pressure describing the operation of the fan. Entries in the first row correspond to the minimum pressure and flow at that pressure for which the fan will operate. For values below this minimum value, flow is assumed to stop. The last row entered by the user corresponds to the highest pressure and flow at that pressure for which the fan will operate. For values above this maximum value, flow is assumed to stop. User specified values are plotted in the pressure-flow plot as red dots. Based on values entered for minimum and maximum pressure, a corresponding regression curve is calculated by the input editor and displayed on the x-y plot as a solid black line. This assists the user in comparing the specified values with the calculated regression curve in order to make appropriate adjustments. Note that only the coefficients calculated for the regression curve are saved to the input file. User specified values are lost after the current CFAST session. Make certain the calculated regression curve is acceptable before saving the input file.

Number of Coefficients: Determines the order of the polynomial fan curve generated using the minimum and maximum pressures and flow at pressures.

47

Regression Coefficients: Coefficients of the polynomial fan curve generated using specified pressures and flows. Polynomials up to order four are permitted. The user may edit individual cell entries to adjust the fan curve displayed in the plot.

Recalculate: This text button enables the user to recalculate the fan curve and corresponding coefficients using the user values in the specified curve spreadsheet. This allows the user to experiment with adjustments to fan curve coefficients with the assurance that the original coefficients can be recalculated.

Values...: This text button displays a spreadsheet window detailing actual points on the calculated regression fan curve. Modifications in this spreadsheet result in a recalculation of the fan curve regression coefficients. This enables the user to iteratively adjust the curve to pass through specified pressure-flow points.

Reverse Direction: Allows the user to reverse the direction of air flow. Flow is indicated on the HVAC overview window flowing from the node indicated with (-) to the node indicated with (+).

2.3.6 Selection of Ceiling Jet Surfaces

Ceiling jet surfaces are specified in the bottom section of the fire scenario overview window. The setting selected by the user applies to the main fire as well as other objects. This affects only the calculation of the convective heating boundary condition for the conduction routines. If a particular surface conduction is *ON* on the compartment geometry window, the ceiling jet algorithm is used to determine the convective heating of the surface. If *OFF*, the bulk temperature of the upper layer determines the convective heating. To select desired ceiling jet settings, click on the pull-down icon to the right of the ceiling jet entry, highlight the desired surface, and click with the mouse or press Enter.

Selections using this pull-down icon affect the CJET key word in the input file.

2.3.7 Specifying Multiple Fires

In addition to the main fire, FAST allows for up to 15 additional buring objects. The object fire window provides for the specification of additional objects to be burned in the fire scenario. The advantage to specifying object fires is that the plume model is separate and distinct from the main fire. In order to specify other objects, select a compartment from the structure graphics list on the fire scenario overview window. Tab or move the mouse to the objects icon, and click or press Enter. The following window is displayed:

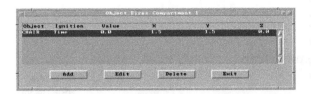

To change the specification for an existing object, highlight the entry and press the Edit button, or double-click on the selection with the mouse. To add a new object, press the Add button. The edit window is displayed.

Note the display of range and measurement units at the bottom of the window as each edit widget is made the focus widget. To customize the units see section 6.2. The OBJECT key word in the input file is affected by changes using this icon.

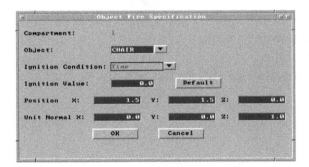

Object: The user may enter the object database key word if known, or may select the object from the database by pressing the pull-down icon. Any object key word entered by the user must exist in the database. By accessing the object from a database, the associated fire curves are predefined and no additional information concerning combustion properties is required.

Ignition Condition: During the simulation, the CFAST model uses the specified condition in combination with the ignition value below to determine if conditions have been met for the object to begin burning. Available conditions include temperature, time, and flux.

Ignition Value: During the simulation, the CFAST model uses the previously specified condition in combination with the ignition value to determine if conditions have been met for the object to begin burning. If the simulation value for this condition exceeds the user specified value for ignition condition, the object starts to burn.

User/Default: This text button determines whether the model obtains the ignition value from the object database entry or from the user specified input in the current input file. If set to *Default*, the model acquires the value from the database allowing the user to change object entries without having to determine the appropriate ignition value for each. If set to *User*, the value entered in the adjacent edit widget is provided to the model. This value must be modified by the user if another object is selected. To toggle the button between *User* and *Default*, click on the button.

For constrained and unconstrained objects only:

X Position: Position of the object as a distance from the rear wall of the compartment. See diagram below.

Y Position: Position of the object as a distance from the left wall of the compartment. See diagram below.

Z Position: Height of the object above the floor of the compartment. See diagram below.

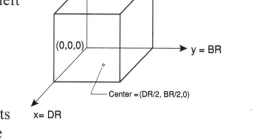

X, Y, and Z Normal Vector: The X, Y, and Z components of the unit normal vector describing the orientation of the object with respect to the back, left corner of the compartment. This should be a unit vector ($X^2 + Y^2 + Z^2 = 1$).

For flame-spread objects only:

Orientation: Database entries for flame-spread objects describe the burning characteristics of the surface, but do not provide orientation of the wall within the compartment. The orientation must be specified for a selected wall object. Available options include *Back Wall*, *Left Wall*, *Right Wall*, and *Front Wall*.

Starting Position: The starting ignition position along the surface of the specified wall. Input is in relation to the back, left corner of the compartment. Based on the orientation of the wall surface previously selected, the input prompts are adjusted to indicate to the user the appropriate X, Y, and Z positions relative to the back, left corner of the compartment. See diagram below.

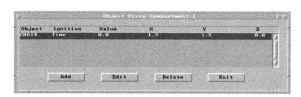

Deleting existing objects: To delete existing objects for a selected compartment, from the selection list, highlight the object to be deleted, and press the Delete button.

2.3.8 Ceiling to Floor Heat Transfer

Ceiling to floor conduction informs the fire model that heat transfer between the ceiling and floor of specified compartments is to be accounted for in the simulation. Ceiling to floor heat transfer occurs between interior compartments of the structure or between an interior compartment and the outdoors.

Ceiling to floor heat transfer is specified by selecting one compartment as the current compartment in the structure graphics list of the fire scenario overview window. The determination of which of a pair of compartments should be selected as the first compartment is not important since specification only enables heat transfer between the compartments. Direction of heat transfer is determined by the temperature characteristics at the time the model is run.

Once a current compartment has been selected, tab or move the mouse to the ceiling/floor conduction icon, and click or press Enter. All compartments with currently defined elevation and height of compartment are displayed in a selection list.

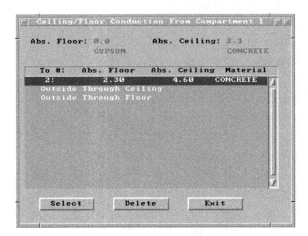

Ceiling to floor heat transfer can only be specified between compartments that could be physically stacked based on specified floor elevations. Some overlap between the absolute floor height of one compartment and the absolute ceiling height of another compartment is allowed. However, whether the compartments are stacked or overlap somewhat, the ceiling and floor absolute elevations must be within .01 meters of each other. In addition, the appropriate ceiling or floor surfaces for the displayed compartment must not have the conduction turned off in the geometry specification window. Those compartments for which such adjacencies are possible, and for which conduction is enabled, are highlighted in white in the selection list. Compartments which cannot be stacked because of these physical constraints have been grayed out. To complete the heat transfer specification, click on the second compartment for which heat transfer is to be enabled and press the Select button, or double-click on the selection with the mouse. The CFCON key word in the input file is affected by changes from this icon.

It is possible to define only one ceiling to floor heat transfer between any pair of internal compartments. Two connections may be specified from a compartment to the outdoors, one through the ceiling and the other through the floor. If the ceiling to floor heat transfer has been enabled for a compartment, the compartment will indicate the specification by the use of shaded lines at the top and bottom of the compartment graphics box.

Deleting existing heat transfer specifications: To delete existing ceiling to floor conduction between a pair of compartments, from the selection list, highlight the compartment to which the heat transfer is to be deleted or disabled, and press the Delete button.

2.3.9 Defining Targets

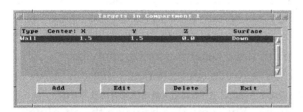 The CFAST model can track and report calculations of the heat flux striking and the temperature of arbitrarily positioned and oriented targets. In order to specify targets, a compartment must be selected from the structure graphics list on the fire scenario overview window. Once a compartment is selected, tab or move the mouse to the target icon, and click or press Enter. The selection list window is displayed.

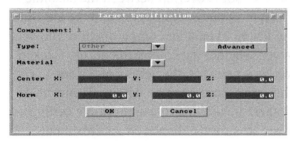 To change the specification for an existing target, highlight the entry and press the Edit button, or double-click on the selection with the mouse. To add a new target, press the Add button. The edit window is displayed.

Note the display of range and measurement units at the bottom of the window as each edit widget is made the focus widget. To customize the units see section 6.2. The TARGET and TARG key words in the input file are affected by changes using this icon, depending on the type of target specified.

Type: The type of target. Two types are provided. The first, *Wall*, is used when the target is one of the walls of the compartment. The second, or *Other*, indicates a target within the compartment.

For wall targets only:

Surface: Specify which of the bounding walls (left, right, front, or back), ceiling (up), or floor (down) is the intended wall target.

X, Y, or Z Center: Based on the wall surface selected above, the input prompts are adjusted to indicate to the user the appropriate X, Y, or Z coordinate axes relative to the back, left corner of the compartment. Specify the target center along the surface of the wall using the indicated coordinate system. See diagram below.

For other targets only:

Material: If non-wall targets are specified, a material must be selected from the thermophysical database to provide heating characteristics of the associated target. This material can be entered by the user or selected from the database. To select a thermophysical material from the database, enter as much of the material database key word as is known, click on the pull-down icon, scroll the database until the desired material is viewed, and select by double-clicking or highlight and

52

press Enter. If a material key word is entered by the user, it must be a valid entry in the thermal properties database.

X Center: Position of the target as a distance from the rear wall of the compartment. See diagram below.

Y Center: Position of the target as a distance from the left wall of the compartment. See diagram below.

Z Center: Height of the target above the floor of the compartment. See diagram below.

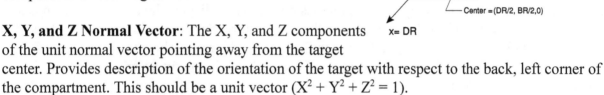

X, Y, and Z Normal Vector: The X, Y, and Z components of the unit normal vector pointing away from the target center. Provides description of the orientation of the target with respect to the back, left corner of the compartment. This should be a unit vector ($X^2 + Y^2 + Z^2 = 1$).

 If a target has been specified for a compartment, the specification will be indicated with a bullseye displayed in the upper right corner of the compartment graphics box on the fire scenario overview window.

Deleting existing targets: To delete existing targets for a selected compartment, from the selection list, highlight the target to be deleted, and press the Delete button.

2.3.10 Modeling Compartment as Shaft

To specify use of a one zone model for individual compartments rather than the typical two zone model, select the compartment from the structure graphics list on the fire scenario overview window. Tab or move the mouse to the geometry icon, and click or press Enter. The edit window for the compartment geometry is displayed.

To specify modeling of the compartment as a shaft, click on the *Model as Shaft* text button and press *OK*.

If a compartment is modeled as a shaft, the specification will be indicated by the use of the * in the upper left corner of the compartment graphics box on the fire scenario overview window.

The SHAFT key word is affected by input using this option.

2.3.11 Selecting Type of Runtime Graphics

For new files, select the *Append Default* graphics option by clicking on the pull-down icon for graphics and selecting the corresponding entry from the list. By selecting this option, a beginning set of runtime graphics descriptors are provided for use by the fire model. If customization of these graphics is desired, it is necessary to edit the input file with a text editor external to the FAST software. This is an advanced feature with details on specific keyword syntax provided in Appendix A.

To change graphics options, click on the graphics pull-down to display the options: *Off*, *Append Default*, *Use Existing*. The *Off* option allows the user to turn graphics off for individual runs of the model. If *Off* is selected and graphics specifications were previously entered, these entries are not lost but have been disabled. Selection of *Use Existing* in the future will make these specifications available again.

2.4 Alternate Databases

Additional databases are provided with each installation of the FAST software, one for thermophysical properties of materials, and two for fire properties of selected common objects (one for multiple burning objects in the CFAST model and one of representative t^2 fires used in the initial selection of the main fire). Functionality is provided to allow advanced users to create their own versions of the thermophysical and objects databases. For the advanced user, the option is available to select alternate thermophysical and object databases. Prior to specifying alternate databases, the user must first generate the new databases following guidelines in sections 2.4.3 to 2.4.5. If the user wants alternate database specifications to pertain to future input sessions, refer to section 2.4.3. If the user wants alternate database specifications to pertain to the current input specifications only, select the filenames icon from the environment section of the fire scenario overview window. The model input / output window is displayed.

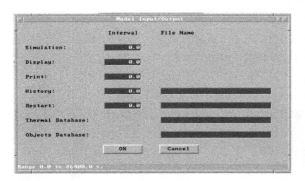

Thermal Database: Name of the thermal properties database used by the geometry window to select materials for different compartment surfaces. This file should have been generated previously according to the sections referenced above.

Objects Database: Name of the objects database used by the other objects fire specification window to select the type of object and associated fire curve information. This file should have been generated previously according to the sections referenced above.

2.4.1 Selecting Default Material

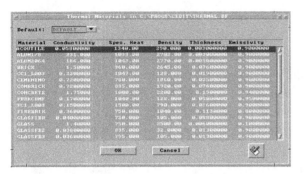

When compartments are added to a structure using the FAST input editor, conduction for wall, ceiling, and floor surfaces are off by default. If the user subsequently turns any of these surfaces on, the material displayed is the system *DEFAULT* material with properties of gypsum wallboard. The user may preselect a material from the thermophysical database which would be used instead of this system *DEFAULT* material. To do this, select *Database* from the desktop menu and select the *Thermophysical* database.

The currently selected default material is displayed next to the *DEFAULT* label. Scroll through the database entries, and select the material desired as the default. Click on the pull-down icon next to the *DEFAULT* label, then click on the *Select Default* option from the menu. Default material selections cannot be saved between uses of the FAST software. Future versions of the program may support permanent selection. To reset to the original *DEFAULT* material setting, click on the pull-down icon next to the *DEFAULT* label, and select the *Reset Default* option from the menu.

2.4.2 Selecting Default Object

When other objects are added to a fire scenario in the FAST input editor, the initial object specification indicates the system *DEFAULT* object with fire properties of plywood. The user may preselect an object from the object database which would be used instead of the system *DEFAULT* object as objects are added. To do this, select *Database* from the desktop menu and select the *Object* database.

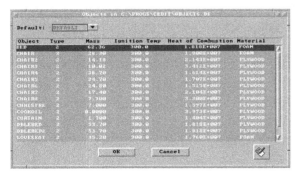

The currently selected default object is displayed next to the *DEFAULT* label. Scroll through the database entries, and select the object desired as the default. Click on the pull-down icon next to the *DEFAULT* label, then click on the *Select Default* option from the menu.

Default object selections cannot be saved between uses of the FAST software. Future versions of the program may support permanent selection. To reset to the original *DEFAULT* object setting, click on the pull-down icon next to the *DEFAULT* label, and select the *Reset Default* option from the menu.

2.4.3 Creating Alternate Databases

It is recommended that users desiring to add new entries use an alternate database rather than adding the entries to either of the databases provided with the software. The thermophysical and object databases provided with the software are frequently revised and recopied to the user disk when upgrades are run. If user specific data has been added to these databases, it could be lost in the upgrade process. To generate alternate databases, select *File Names* from the desktop menu.

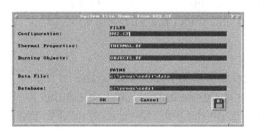

Enter the name of the alternate database under the *FILES* section of the window for either the thermophysical or burning objects database. If the specified database file(s) are to be used every time the FAST software is run, click on the disk icon in the lower right corner of the window. This saves current settings to the configuration file indicated in both the window title and the first edit widget.

If the specified database file(s) are to be used only for the current FAST software run, click on the *OK* button and continue with input following the guidelines in either section 2.4.4 or section 2.4.5 below corresponding to the type of database being generated.

2.4.4 Editing Thermophysical Database

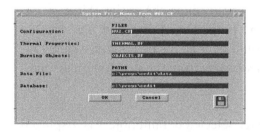

Functionality is provided to allow users to add new entries to specified thermophysical databases, change or delete existing entries, and rebuild the database and corresponding index structures. Prior to selecting any of these options, the user must first indicate the database file to which the modifications are to be applied. From the desktop menu, select *Options* then select *File Names*.

If the thermophysical database file to be edited is stored in a directory other than the database directory displayed in the *PATHS* section of the window, enter the new path next to the *Database* label. Enter the thermophysical database filename next to the *Thermal Properties* label in the *FILES* section of the window, and click on the *OK* button. Do not click on the files icon unless this database file name is to become the default thermophysical database for all future uses of the software.

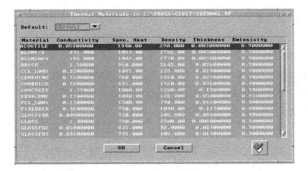

From the desktop menu, select *Database* then select *Thermophysical*.

To add new entries or change existing entries in the database, click on the editor icon.

Select the appropriate option, *Add* or *Change* from the menu displayed.

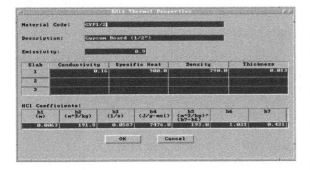

If editing an existing entry, the current database code and details are displayed. If adding a new entry, no database code is provided, and only default values are displayed. Note the display of range and measurement units at the bottom of the window as each edit widget is made the focus widget. To customize the units see section 6.2. Enter details following guidelines for each input prompt. Values entered for the material are not saved to the database file until the user clicks on the *OK* button.

Material Code: From 1 to 8 alphanumeric characters, used to uniquely identify this entry within the database.

Description: Detailed description of material. Provide sufficient information to distinguish similar materials from one another.

Emissivity: Emissivity of the exposed surface, compartment interior, of the material. Dimensionless.

The next four properties support up to three layers, or slabs, per partition. The layers are numbered from the inside to the outside of the material. That is, the first material property represents the material on the compartment interior, and the last property is on the outside.

Conductivity: Display units dependent on user selections for base measurements: energy absorption rate/length/temperature.

Specific Heat: Display units dependent on user selections for base measurements: energy/mass/temperature.

Density: Display units dependent on user selections for base measurements: mass/cubic length.

Thickness: Display units dependent on user selections for base measurements: length.

HCl Coefficients: There are seven coefficients for the HCl absorption. If the first two are zero, the others are not used. These coefficients have only been measured for a few materials and are discussed in more detail in reference [45]. Units for each coefficient are specified in the corresponding spreadsheet headings and cannot be modified by the user.

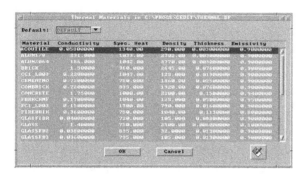

Deleting Materials: From the thermophysical database entry selection window.

Click on the editor icon, and select the *Delete* option. A confirming message window is displayed.

Respond *Yes* to delete, *Cancel* to return to selection window without deleting.

Rebuilding Database: From the thermophysical database entry selection window, click on the editor icon, and select the *Rebuild* option. A confirming message window is displayed.

Respond *Yes* to rebuild database and corresponding index file, *Cancel* to return to selection window without rebuilding.

2.4.5 Editing Object Database

Functionality is provided to allow users to add new entries to specified object databases, change or delete existing entries, and rebuild the database and corresponding index structures. Prior to selecting any of these options, the user must first indicate the database file to which the modifications are to be applied. From the desktop menu, select *Options* then select *File Names*.

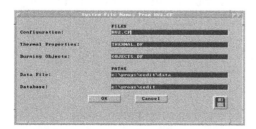

If the object database file to be edited is stored in a directory other than the database directory displayed in the *PATHS* section of the window, enter the new path next to the *Database* label. Enter the object database filename next to the *Burning Objects* label in the *FILES* section of the window, and click on the *OK* button. Do not click on the files icon unless this database file name is to become the default object database for all future uses of the software.

From the desktop menu, select *Database* then select *Object*. To add new entries or change existing entries in the database, click on the editor icon.

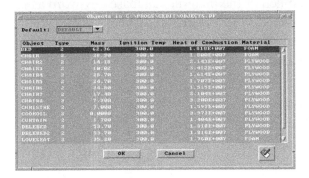

Select the appropriate option, *Add* or *Change* from the menu displayed. The following window is displayed:

If editing an existing entry, the current database code and details are displayed. If adding a new entry, no database code is provided, and only default values are displayed. Note the display of range and measurement units at the bottom of the window as each edit widget is made the focus widget. To customize the units see section 6.2. Enter details following guidelines for each input prompt. Details for the object are not saved to the database file until the user clicks on the *OK* button.

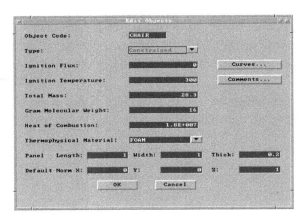

Object Code: From 1 to 8 alphanumeric characters, used to uniquely identify this entry within the database.

Type: Three types are supported: unconstrained, constrained (default for new entries), and flame spread. Not all inputs below are available for all types. If an unconstrained type is selected, only the toxic combustion products can be specified for species time curves. All other species curves are available for a constrained object type. If flame spread type is specified, panel dimensions and normal vector coordinates are not available for input.

Ignition Flux: Flux for ignition. Display units dependent on user selections for base measurements: energy absorption rate/length^2.

Ignition Temperature: Temperature for ignition. Display units dependent on user selections for base measurements: temperature.

Total Mass: Display units dependent on user selections for base measurements: mass.

Gram Molecular Weight: Gram molecular weight.

Heat of Combustion: Display units dependent on user selections for base measurements: energy/mass.

59

Thermophysical Material: Material from the thermophysical database used when user has specified object as an ambient target in order to provide thermophysical properties to the model. This material can be entered by the user or selected from the database. To select a thermophysical material from the database, enter as much of the material database key word as is known, click on the pull-down icon, scroll the database until the desired material is viewed, and select by double-clicking, or highlight and press Enter. If the material key word is entered by the user, it must be a valid entry in the thermal properties database before the object entry can be updated.

For constrained and unconstrained objects only:

Panel Length: Panel length.

Panel Width: Panel width.

Panel Height: Panel height.

X, Y, and Z Default Normal: The X, Y, and Z components of the unit normal vector describing the orientation of the object with respect to the back, left corner of a compartment. These values are provided as defaults when object is selected by the user in the fire scenario definition.

Curves...: This text button provides access to additional windows for defining object fire curves. The actual curves available are dependent on the type of object. See subsection 2.4.5.1 below for a complete discussion of the object curves.

Comments...: This text button provides access to an additional window for specifying user comments. See subsection 2.4.5.2 below for a complete discussion of the object comments.

Flame Spread...: This text button provides access to an additional window for specifying flame spread properties, and is only available for a flame spread type object. See subsection 2.4.5.2 below for a complete discussion of the flame spread properties.

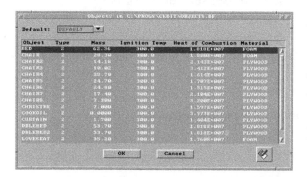

Deleting Objects: From the object database entry selection window, click on the editor icon, and select the *Delete* A confirming message window is displayed.

Respond *Yes* to delete, *Cancel* to return to selection window without deleting.

Rebuilding Database: From the object database entry selection window, click on

60

the editor icon, and select the *Rebuild* option. A confirming message window is displayed.

Respond *Yes* to rebuild database and corresponding index file, *No* to return to selection window without rebuilding.

2.4.5.1 Object Fire Curves

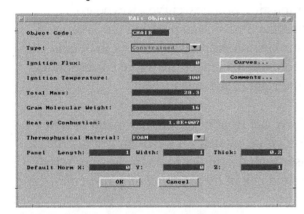

To define a time-dependent fire curve, the user must first access the object entry from the database and display the detail window following the guidelines in section 2.4.5 above.

Fire height, fire area, heat release rate, and pyrolysis rate are available for all fire types. If the selected object is an unconstrained fire type, only the toxic combustion products are available for species curves.

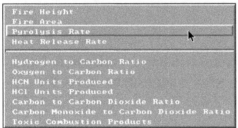

Tab or move the mouse to the *Curves...* text button, and click or press Enter. A selection menu is displayed.

Select the desired curve, *e.g.*, *Pyrolysis Rate*, from the menu.

A window similar to the following is displayed. The actual title for the window depends on the curve selected from the previous menu. Note the display of range and measurement units at the bottom of the window as each cell in the edit list widget is made the focus widget. To customize the units see section 6.2. If no other time-

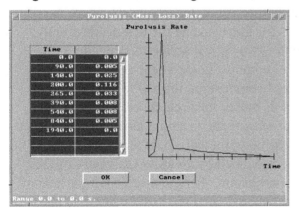

dependent curves have been entered previously for this object entry, no entries will be displayed in the spreadsheet. To enter time curves for the first time, Tab to the spreadsheet or click on the first cell using the mouse. Enter the actual time at which each fire property is evaluated. Use the vertical scrollbar to enter additional entries beyond those initially displayed. Refer to the GUI Terminology section 1.3.2 of this reference guide for an explanation of the use of scrollbars in the GUI interface.

Movement between time cells is handled using the ↑ and ↓ keys. To insert a new time entry between two existing rows, press Alt-i. To delete a row, press Alt-d. Deleting a row moves all rows following the deleted row up one row. If the entry is to be erased, but all other rows are to remain in current positions, press Alt-e to erase the row. Time entry value ranges are constrained by the entries in surrounding time cells so that time entries within a column of the spreadsheet are ever increasing values. The maximum value allowed is 86400 seconds. Once time entries have been completed for one curve, these timepoints are available for all other curves. Consequently, only the y-axis values will need to be entered for subsequent curves.

Once the time points have been specified in the first column of the curve spreadsheet, select the top cell of the right column to begin entering the combustion property curve. Keyboard movement from the time column can be handled using the Shift-→ and pressing the ↑ key until the first cell is reached. Specify the values for the combustion property according to details discussed below. As values are entered in the right column, the object fire curve corresponding to time and y-axis entries is plotted on the graph to the right of the spreadsheet.

Fire Height: The height of the base of the flames above the floor of the compartment of fire origin. The values entered are added to the z-position value entered for the main fire in order to determine the exact fire height. This provides the user with the ability to define an appropriate shape for the fire height curve, and then adjust the actual height by changing only one entry, the z position, as opposed to modifying all entries in the curve.

Fire Area: The area of the fire at the base of the flames.

Pyrolysis Rate: The rate at which fuel is pyrolyzed at times corresponding to each point of the specified object fire. Note concerns below regarding the overspecification of the object fire curves.

Heat Release Rate: The heat release rate of the object fire. Note concerns below regarding the overspecification of the object fire curves.

Overspecifying Object Fire Curves: If each of the three parameters, heat of combustion from the object detail window, heat release rate curve, and pyrolysis rate have been specified, the object fire is overspecified. The input editor accounts for this by using the two most recently entered to calculate the third parameter. This allows for two typical scenarios depending on whether the user desires to use a constant value heat of combustion or a heat of combustion curve. If the user desires to use a constant value heat of combustion, this value should first be entered in the object detail window. Either the pyrolysis rate or heat release rate curve is then entered. If the pyrolysis rate curve is entered, the heat release rate is automatically calculated by multiplying each entry in the pyrolysis rate curve by the constant value heat of combustion. If the heat release rate is entered, the pyrolysis rate curve is calculated by dividing each entry of the heat release rate curve by the constant value heat of combustion. For the user desiring a heat of combustion curve rather than a constant value, the user should enter the heat release rate and pyrolysis rate curves separately. The model will calculate the appropriate heat of combustion curve prior to execution. One caution regarding this approach. If a user desiring a constant value heat of combustion saves the entry and returns later, the input editor views the heat release rate and pyrolysis rate curves as the last two properties entered. If the user then makes modifications to entries in one of the curves, the other curve will not be automatically calculated. It is necessary to make a change to the heat of combustion in order to get the second curve recalculated.

Hydrogen to Carbon Ratio: The mass ratio of hydrogen to carbon as it becomes available from the fuel. Units are kg/kg.

Oxygen to Carbon Ratio: The mass ratio of oxygen to carbon as it becomes available from the fuel. Units are kg/kg.

HCN Units Produced: Kilogram of hydrogen cyanide produced per kilogram of fuel pyrolized.

HCL Units Produced: Kilogram of hydrogen chloride produced per kilogram of fuel pyrolized.

Carbon to Carbon Dioxide Ratio: Ratio of the mass of carbon to carbon dioxide produced by the oxidation of the fuel. This curve is used to simulate soot production.

Carbon Monoxide to Carbon Dioxide Ratio: Ratio of the mass of carbon monoxide to carbon dioxide produced by the oxidation of the fuel.

Toxic Combustion Products: Kilogram of "toxic" combustion products produced per kilogram of fuel pyrolized.

2.4.5.2 Object Comments

The FAST software supports entry of up to three comments for each object in the database. To enter comments, the user must first access the object entry from the database and display the detail window following the guidelines in section 2.4.5 above.

Tab or move the mouse to the *Comments...* text button, and click or press Enter.

Enter comments in any of the three text edit widgets provided. Select *OK* to accept these entries or *Cancel* to return to the detail window with previous comment entries unchanged.

63

2.4.5.3 Flame Spread Object Properties

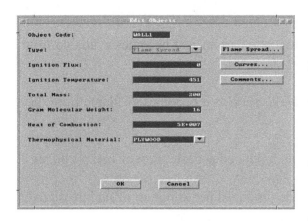

Entry of flame spread object properties is only available for objects specified in the database as flame spread type. To enter properties, the user must first access the object entry from the database and display the detail window following the guidelines in section 2.4.5 above.

If the object is a flame spread type, a *Flame Spread* button is displayed. Type must be set to flame spread to make the button visible and accessible. Tab or move the mouse to the *Flame Spread...* text button, and click or press Enter.

Note the display of range and measurement units at the bottom of the window as each edit widget is made the focus widget. To customize the units see section 6.2. Enter details following guidelines for each input prompt.

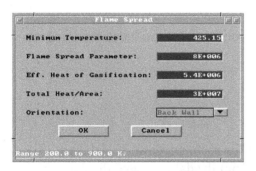

Minimum Temperature: Minimum temperature for lateral flame spread. Obtained from the Lateral Ignition and Flame spread Test apparatus or LIFT.

Flame Spread Parameter: Obtained from the Lateral Ignition and Flame spread Test apparatus or LIFT.

Eff. Heat of Combustion: The effective heat of combustion of the object.

Total Heat/Area: Total heat released per unit area.

Orientation: Orientation of wall within a compartment. Available options include *Back Wall*, *Left Wall*, *Right Wall*, and *Front Wall*.

Select *OK* to accept these entries or *Cancel* to return to the detail window with previous flame spread entries unchanged.

2.5 Alternate Configuration Files

By default, settings for measurement display units, directories, and database filenames are stored in configuration file provided with the FAST installation. The software supports alternate

64

configurations of these quantities which enable the user to vary setup by project or other groupings. To change the name of the configuration file used for the current input session, select *File Names* from the desktop menu.

Enter the name of the alternate configuration file under the *FILES* section of the window. If the specified configuration file exists, measurement display units and directory paths are updated to reflect those entries in that configuration file. If the specified configuration file does not exist, measurement display units are set to SI values by default, directory searches are local to the current directory, and the thermophysical and objects database entries reference the databases supplied with the FAST software. Modifications can be made following the guidelines in sections 6.1, 6.2, and 2.4.3. To save these settings for future use, click on the disk icon in the lower right corner of the window. This saves current settings to the configuration file now indicated in both the window title and the first edit widget.

2.6 Running the Simple Example

Once the description of the fire scenario is complete, the fire scenario overview window is displayed. This window enables the user to see at a glance the major characteristics of the scenario prior to running the simulation. It is possible to quickly determine the number of compartments (# of boxes drawn in structure section of window), the fire compartment (red box), and compartments with some type of sprinkler or detector (cyan or light blue boxes).

To run the simulation, use the mouse to select the *Run Simulation* icon. After selecting the Run Simulation icon, a window is displayed prompting for times at which the simulation is to pause. These times can be relative to the beginning of the simulation or to the operation of a detection device. For this example, Click on *OK* to indicate no pauses and begin the simulation.

The results of the simulation are displayed in the simulation status window. As the calculation proceeds, the display is updated. The current simulation time is displayed along with calculated values for temperatures, layer interface height, and major gas species.

Graphs of temperature, layer interface height, and heat release rate can also be displayed by clicking on the *Graph* button.

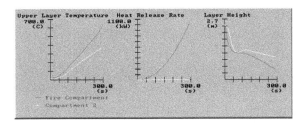

For this example, flashover is reached in approximately 400 s. At this point, the simulation is paused enabling the user to modify the fire description to include the burning of additional combustibles in the compartment. Additionally, the sizes of vents may be changed. For this example, simply click on the *Stop* button to end the simulation. The *Print Report* (to print a summary of the input data and model calculations) and *Print Graph* (to print the three graphs to printers which support the HPGL graphics format) buttons can be used to produce printed documentation of the simulation. For this example, select *Close* to return to the fire scenario overview window.

This completes the example. Additional details on running a scenario are included in section 3. To exit FAST, use the mouse to select the desktop icon and display the desktop menu Select the *File* options, then select *Quit*. Since a new simulation has been created and not saved to disk, a window is displayed to allow the option of saving the file prior to exiting the program. Since this example can easily be recreated following the instructions above and is already included as EXMEDIUM.DAT, click on *No* to exit the program without saving a data file to disk.

2.7 Recommended Procedure for Defining New Files

Once the number of compartments and fire type have been specified for the new file, the fire scenario overview window is displayed. The user is free to enter information in any order desired with the constraint that compartments should be specified first. As an aid in generating an input file for the first time user, the following sequence is suggested:

- Enter a title for the input file.

- Enter the ambient conditions.

- Specify output files and intervals for acquiring information during the fire model run.

- **SAVE THE FILE**

- Modify compartment geometries for all compartments.

- **SAVE THE FILE**

- Modify and / or define horizontal and vertical connections.

66

- **SAVE THE FILE**

- Modify and / or define mechanical ventilation connections.

- **SAVE THE FILE**

- Position sprinklers and detectors in appropriate compartments.

- **SAVE THE FILE**

- Position fire.

- Modify detailed time curves for the fire including species production, heat release rate, and pyrolysis rate.

- **SAVE THE FILE**

2.8 Opening and Saving Input Files

2.8.1 Selecting an Existing Input File

It is recommended that the new user run through the simple example provided above to gain familiarity with the layout of the overview windows in the input editor. Once the user is familiar with the layout, new input files can be quickly generated following the guidelines in section 2.8.2.

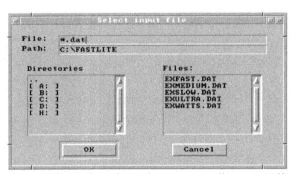

In order to view an existing FAST input file, select the *File* option from the desktop menu in the FAST GUI shell, then select *Open*. A file specification window is displayed.

The file specification window consists of four key elements: the filename edit widget, the directory edit widget, the directory selection list, and the filename selection list. To search directories other than the current directory displayed in the directory edit widget, enter the new directory name in the directory edit widget and press Enter. Directories may also be selected by double-clicking on the drive or directory in the directory selection list. If the filename is known, enter it in the filename edit widget and press Enter. Do not include the drive or directory in the filename. Drive and directory specifications are handled only through the directory edit widget and the directory selection list widget. If a partial filename is known, enter the known characters along with * to indicate those parts of the filename for which characters are not known. For example, enter *t*.dat* and press Enter to select data file beginning with the letter *t*. All files matching the specified file name are displayed in the filename selection list. Use the mouse to double-click on the filename desired in the selection list, or highlight the name and click on the *OK* button.

2.8.2 Creating a New Input File

Using the mouse, click on *File* and *New* to begin the definition of a new fire scenario. Initially, there are two steps to defining a new fire scenario to be modeled – selection of the geometry of the structure (the number of compartments and connections between the compartments) and a description of the fire.

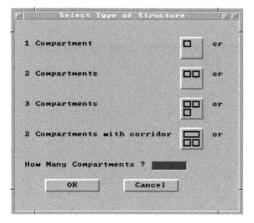

Once *New* is selected, the structure selection window is displayed. From this window, the number of compartments and the arrangement of the compartments is defined. Once an initial selection has been made, the size of the compartments and any connections between compartments can be customized to fit the details of a specific scenario. Use the mouse to select one of the compartment icons (1 compartment, 2 compartments, 3 compartments, or 2 compartments with a corridor). Note that the selection highlights the icon with a bold black border. Each of these four selections creates a structure with an appropriate number of compartments, doors between the compartments and leakage to the outside.

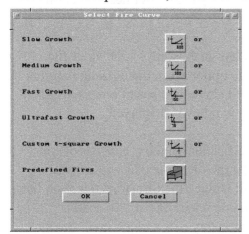

Alternatively, by selecting "How many compartments?" the use can create a structure without defining any ventilation. This later option is useful for creating customized structures for specific known scenarios. Click on *OK* to close the window.

Following selection of the structure, the fire is specified. For a wide range of fires, the fire growth can be accurately represented with a power law relation of the form

$$\dot{Q} \propto \alpha \, t^2 \tag{3}$$

where $\dot{Q}$ is the heat release rate of the fire, α is the fire intensity coefficient, and *t* is time. A set of specific T-squared fires labeled slow, medium, fast, and ultra-fast fires with fire intensity coefficients (α) such that the fires reached 1055 kW (1000 BTU/s) in 600 s, 300 s, 150 s, and 75 s, respectively are predefined within FAST. In addition, a custom growth rate can also be selected.

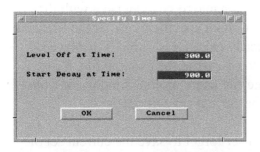

Use the mouse to select one of the fire growth rate icons (slow growth, medium growth, fast growth, ultra-fast growth, custom t-squared growth, or predefined fires). Note that the selection highlights the icon with a bold black border. Click on *OK* to close the window. The Specify Times window is displayed. This window takes two forms.

If one of the standard fire growth rate curves is selected (slow, medium, fast, or ultra-fast), a window is displayed to input a time to the end of the growth phase of the fire (a "Level Off at Time" input) and of the steady burning phase of the fire (a "Start Decay at Time" input) can be defined. If the custom t-squared growth curve is selected, the window also includes the beginning time for fire growth, the time to reach 1 MW and the time at the end of the decay phase of the fire.

If desired, the default times can be changed by selecting one of the edit widgets and using the keyboard to change the number to any desired value. Click on *OK* to accept the chosen values and close the window.

If the predefined fire is selected, a selection list window is display with a description of a number of fire scenarios taken from the literature [32], [46], [47]. Select one of the entries with the mouse and click on *OK* to accept the chosen entry and close the window. This completes the description of the fire scenario.

2.8.3 Saving Input File Modifications

In order to reuse input specifications from one use of the FAST software to another, the user must request the input editor to store the information on the computer's hard disk. All information for the current session of the input editor is grouped together on the hard disk and assigned a unique name referred to as the filename for retrieval purposes in the future. It is strongly recommended that input file specifications be frequently saved to disk as outlined in section 2.7. Two options are available for saving input to disk depending on whether the previous set of information is to be retained or replaced. If an existing input file was opened and modifications made, the user may replace the previous specifications with the new specifications by clicking on the diskette icon and selecting the *Save* option. If the previous set of specifications may be needed in the future, select the *Save As* option.

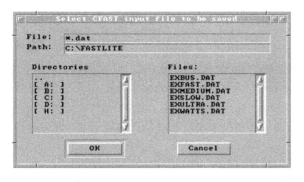

Enter a unique name to be associated with the current set of input specifications. If the filename entered already exists, a warning is displayed. Select *Yes* to overwrite the existing file, *No* to return to the file name prompt window, or *Cancel* to cancel the current save as operation.

Should the user forget to save the current set of specifications prior to exiting the FAST shell, a warning box is displayed. Select *Yes* to save the file, *No* to exit without saving the file, or *Cancel* to return to the GUI shell.

3 Running the Fire Model

3.1 Starting the Simulation

 When the description of a fire scenario is completed or an existing file is opened, the fire scenario overview window is displayed. At this point the simulation can be started. To begin the simulation, use the mouse to click on the *Run Simulation* icon.

Before beginning the simulation, a window is displayed to allow the user the option to pause the simulation. The default is to have the simulation run to completion. To activate a pause condition, click on the button associated with the condition to switch it from *No* to *Yes*. Enter the time desired in the corresponding edit field. None, one, or both conditions can be set. Once the pause conditions are set as desired click on *OK* to begin the simulation. Selecting *Cancel* will end the simulation and return to the fire scenario overview window.

Pause at Time: The simulation can be paused at a specific user defined time. This allows existing vents to be opened or closed at some point during the simulation. An example of using this feature is given in section 3.

Pause After Detector: The simulation can also be paused at a specified time relative to detector activation. This feature allows for the simulation of automatic doors that close when a detector activates or some other action in response to a detector. If more than one detector is included in a simulation, the pause time applies to all detectors.

Pause at Heat Flux Warning: The simulation can also be paused at a user specified heat flux at the center of the floor of the fire compartment. This can be used as another indicator of flashover (values in the range of the default of 20 kW/m² are typically used to represent impending flashover) or as an indicator of pain or burns to persons exposed to the fire. For example, a heat flux of 84 kW/m² for a duration of 17 s is included in the NFPA standard for protection apparel for firefighters.

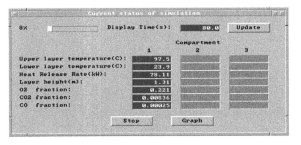

3.2 While the Simulation Runs

Once the simulation starts, the simulation status window is displayed. The simulation time and other information are automatically updated at intervals specified by the user (in the output file window covered in section 2.3.5). For each

71

compartment the upper layer temperature, lower layer temperature, total heat release rate, fraction of O_2, fraction CO_2 and fraction of CO are listed in a column.

Update: Click on the *Update* button to display the current conditions on the simulation status window and the graph window if selected.

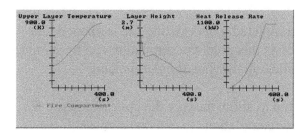

Graph: The graph button controls the display of a window showing graphs of the upper layer temperature, the calculated HRR, and the upper layer depth. Once the graph window is displayed clicking on the graph button closes the graph window. In the lower left corner of the graph window is the legend for all three graphs. The fire room is always the red line so that it is easy to identify. When the update button is clicked on the graphs are also updated.

Stop: The stop button does as the name implies. It terminates the simulation closes the status window and the graph window if it is open and returns to the fire scenario window.

3.3 Handling Events During the Simulation

Several events can cause the simulation to pause. The first three are in response to inputs from the pause window at the start of the simulation. Finally, the simulation may be paused when flashover conditions are reached – when the upper layer in the fire room reaches 600 °C.

At either the time specified to pause the model, the specified time relative to detector activation, or the time when the heat flux at floor level exceeds a user specified value, a window is displayed with notification of the reason for the pause and offering three options. From left to right are *Modify*, *Continue*, and *Stop*. *Modify* allows the user to change the size of any predefined vent – see below for details. *Continue* returns to the simulation to continue running. *Stop* terminates the simulation and returns to the fire scenario window.

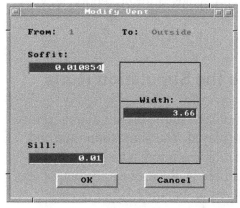

Modify Vents The *Modify* button displays a window listing all the vents available. Only vents that already exist can be changed, new ones cannot be added. A vent can be selected to be modified either one of two ways. First the mouse cursor can be positioned over the vent and selected. Then clicking on the *modify* button goes to the modify window. The other method is to simply double click on the desired vent in the list. The *continue* button starts the simulation back.

72

The window for modifying a particular vent in the simulation has three fields for data. The top one gives the current height of the soffit of the vent relative to the floor. The middle field has the width of the vent and the bottom has the height of the sill. All three fields can be edited to change that particular characteristic of the vent. *Ok* returns to the modify vent window saving any new inputs. The *cancel* button returns without changing the values the simulation is using.

Finally, the simulation may be paused when flashover conditions are reached – when the upper layer in the fire room reaches 600 °C. When this happens, a window is displayed informing that flashover has occurred and allows the user to continue the simulation or to stop. *Continue* allows the simulation to proceed with the user defined fire. *Modify Parameters* allows the user to change any existing parameters for post-flashover burning. *Modify Vents* allows the user to change the size of any predefined vent. *Stop* terminates the simulation and returns to the fire scenario overview window.

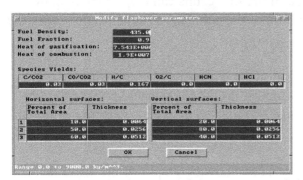

Flashover: Clicking the *Modify Parameters* button displays the flashover screen. The flashover screen has a number for entries of information needed to continue the simulation in flashover. Default values are provided for every field.

Fuel density: Average density of the fuel burning during post-flashover burning

Fuel fraction: the fraction of the total material that will pyrolyze and lead to combustion.

Heat of gasification: the amount of energy necessary to pyrolyze a unit mass of the fuel – that is turn it from a solid to a gas.

Heat of combustion: the amount of energy a given mass of the fuel gives off when it burns.

Combustion chemistry: The next row of entries defines the combustion chemistry for the fuel. *C/CO2* field is the ratio of mass of carbon produced for smoke to the mass of carbon dioxide produced in combustion of the fuel. *CO/CO2* is the ratio of mass of CO produced to the mass of CO2 produced in combustion of the fuel. *H/C* is the ratio of the mass of hydrogen to carbon in the fuel. *O2/C* is the mass of oxygen liberated to the atmosphere by pyrolization to the mass of carbon in the fuel. *HCN* and *HCl* are the ratio of the mass of HCN and HCl produced to the mass of CO2 in combustion.

Available fuel: These tables are used to put in the amount of fuel available in the room. One table is for fuel with its surface oriented horizontally; the other is for fuel with its surface oriented vertically. For each orientation, up to three thicknesses of fuel can be specified. The amount of fuel is given as a percentage of the total room surface with the same orientation. For example, for horizontal fuel, this is the percentage of the total wall surface area. The area in a table can add up to more than 100 percent to allow for the inclusion of surface area of furniture, partitions, or other material in the compartment. When all the inputs are satisfactory clicking on the *OK* button continues the run.

3.4   Saving the Results of the Simulation

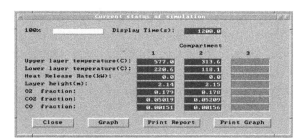

When the simulation is complete, the results of the calculations are available in several forms. If spreadsheet output was selected (see section 2.2.2 for details on specifying spreadsheet output), the user-specified file can be imported into a spreadsheet or other program for further analysis. In addition, the results can be printed in tabular or graphical form. Four buttons are available at the bottom of the simulation status window once the simulation is complete:

Close: Select *Close* to close the simulation status window (and associated graph window if displayed) and return to the fire scenario overview window. If *Close* is selected prior to the *Print Report* and/or *Print Graph*, below, the simulation must be repeated to be able to print the tabular report or graph.

Graph: The *Graph* button controls the display of a window showing graphs of the upper layer temperature, the calculated HRR, and the upper layer depth. Once the graph window is displayed clicking on the graph button closes the graph window.

Print Report: Select the *Print Report* button to produce a printed summary of the input file and the results of the simulation.

Print Graph: Select the *Print Graph* button to produce a printed copy of the three graphs displayed with the *Graph* button, above. Printed graphs are only available on printers which support the HPGL graphics language. This includes all Hewlett-Packard LaserJet printers beginning with the LaserJet III. For other printers, consult the printer documentation to see if your printer supports the HPGL graphics language.

4 An Advanced Example

This section provides an example using FAST which simulates an actual fire incident. Since the input is more complex than the example presented earlier, the user should be familiar with the use of FAST prior to working this example.

4.1 The Incident

On March 28, 1994, the New York City Fire Department (FDNY) responded to a report of smoke and sparks issuing from a chimney at a three story apartment building in Manhattan. The officer in charge ordered three-person hose teams to make entry into the first- and second-floor apartments while the truck company ventilated the stairway from the roof. When the door to the first-floor apartment was forced open, a large flame issued from the apartment and up the stairway, engulfing the three firefighters at the second floor landing. The flame persisted for at least 6½ minutes, resulting in their deaths. The FDNY requested the assistance of the National Institute of Standards and Technology (NIST) to model the incident in the hope of understanding the factors which produced a backdraft condition of such a duration.

The Building: The fire occurred in a three story, multiple brick dwelling of ordinary construction approximately 6.1 m (20 ft) wide by 14 m (46 ft) deep, and 3½ stories tall. The building contained four apartments, one on each story, with the basement apartment half below grade. While the basement apartment had its own entrance, access to the others was by an enclosed stairway running up the side of the building. The building was attached to an identical building that was not involved.

The buildings were built in the late 1800's and had undergone many alterations over the years. Recent renovations included replacement of the plaster/lathe with drywall on wood studs, lowering the ceilings to 2.5 m (8.25 ft), new windows and doors, heavy thermal insulation, sealing and calking to minimize air infiltration (the building was described as very tight.). Built before central heat, the apartments had numerous fireplaces, most of which had been sealed. The apartment of fire origin had two fireplaces, but only the one in the living room was operable. All apartments had thick plank wood floors.

The apartments had similar floor plans; the differences resulting from the stairway. A floor plan of the first floor apartment is presented in figure 2. There was a living room in the front, kitchen and bathroom in the center, and a bedroom in the rear. Not found in the other apartments, the first floor apartment had an office within the bedroom which was not significant in the fire. The roof had a scuttle for access and a wired glass skylight located over the stairway.

The Fire: On March 28, 1994 at 7:36 p.m., the New York City Fire Department received a telephone report of heavy smoke and sparks coming from a chimney at 62 Watts St., Manhattan. The initial response was 3 engines, 2 ladders, and a battalion chief. On arrival they saw the smoke from the chimney but no other signs of fire. The engine companies were assigned to ventilate the roof above the stairs by opening the scuttle and skylight, and two three-person hose teams advanced lines through the main entrance to the first- and second-floor apartment doors.

The first-floor hose team forced the apartment door and reported:

> a momentary rush of air into the apartment, followed by
> a warm (but not hot) exhaust, followed by
> a large flame issuing from the upper part of the door and extending up the stairway.

The first-floor team was able to duck down under the flame and retreat down the stairs, but the three men at the second-floor level were engulfed by the flame which now filled the stairway. An amateur video was being taken from across the street and became an important source of information when later reviewed by the fire department. This showed the flame filling the stairway and venting out the open scuttle and skylight, extending well above the roof of the building. Further, the video showed that the flame persisted at least 6½ minutes (the tape had several pauses of unknown duration, but there was 6½ minutes of tape showing the flame).

Damage to the apartment of origin was limited to the living room, kitchen and hall -- closed doors prevented fire spread to the bedroom, bath, office, and closets. There was no fire extension to the other apartments and no structural damage. The wired glass in the skylight was melted in long "icicles" and the wooden stairs were mostly consumed. The description provided by the surviving hose team was of a classic backdraft; but these usually persist only seconds before exhausting their fuel supply. Where did the fuel come from to feed this flame for so long?

Cause and Origin: The subsequent investigation revealed that the first-floor occupant went out at 6:25 p.m., leaving a plastic trash bag atop the (gas) kitchen range which he was sure was turned off. It is reasonable that the pilot light ignited the bag, which then involved several bottles of high alcohol content liquor on the counter, and spread the fire to the wood floor and other contents. The occupant confirmed that all doors and windows were closed, so that the only source of combustion air was the fireplace flue in the living room from which the smoke and sparks were seen to emerge.

4.2 Computer Analysis

Clearly, the fire burned for nearly an hour under severely vitiated conditions. The open flue initially provided expansion relief and later vented smoke as the ceiling layer dropped below the level of the opening. Such vitiated combustion results in the production of large quantities of unburned fuel and high CO/CO_2 ratios. As shown in studies of the backdraft phenomenon, when a door is opened under such conditions, warm air flowing out is replaced by ambient air which carries oxygen to the fuel. When this combustible mixture ignites, a large flame extends from the door. To determine whether enough fuel could collect within the apartment to feed the flame for the period of time observed, FAST was used to recreate the incident.

The apartment of origin was modeled as a single room with dimensions of 6.1 m by 14 m by 2.5 m. The stairway was modeled as a second room 1.2 m by 3 m by 9.1 m connected to the apartment by a closed door and having a vent at the roof of 0.84 m^2 area. The fireplace flue was modeled as a small leakage opening at the height of the top of the fireplace opening .

The initial fire was assumed to be a constant heat release rate (HRR) of 25 kW from actual data on burning trash bags. This fire then transitioned into a "medium growth rate t-squared" fire with a peak heat release rate of 1MW; however this was reached only momentarily due to limited oxygen. Such "medium t2" fires are characteristic of most common items of residential contents.

4.3 Entering the Data

To start FAST, change to the directory which contains the program and run it by changing to the directory where the software was installed and executing the program. The following commands are typical:

```
cd \FAST
FAST
```

from the DOS command prompt (pressing the Enter key after each command). After the FAST logo appears, the main desktop menu is displayed. Using the mouse, click on *File* and *New* to begin the definition of a new fire scenario.

Once *New* is selected, the structure selection window is displayed. From this window, the number of compartments and the arrangement of the compartments is defined. Once an initial selection has been made, the size of the compartments and any connections between compartments will be customized to fit the details of this specific scenario. For this example, choose a two compartment example by using the mouse to select the "2 Compartments" icon. Note that the selection highlights the icon with a bold black border. This selection defines two 2.4 m wide by 3.6 m deep by 2.4 m high compartments with connecting doorways. These dimensions will be customized to fit the current building geometry below. For now, click on *OK* to accept the selection and close the window.

For this example, a customized medium T-squared growth rate fire will be specified. In a mixed

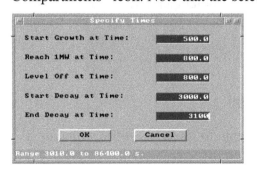

collection of fuels selecting the medium curve is appropriate as long as there is no especially flammable item present. In a manner similar to the selection of the 2 compartment structure geometry above, select the custom growth rate fire by using the mouse to select the "Custom Growth" icon. Note that the selection highlights the icon with a bold black border. Click on *OK* to close the window. A window is displayed to define critical time points for the fire. For this example, enter 300 s and 3000 s respectively. Click on *OK* to accept these values and close the window. This fire description will be further customized to fit the current fire scenario below.

For this test case, typical metric units will be used. Select *Options* from the desktop menu, then

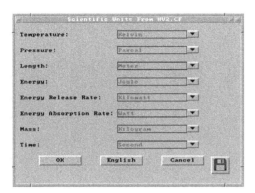

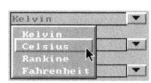

selecting *User Specified Units* to display the measurement units window. To modify the settings for any of the base measurements, click on the pull-down icon to the right of the measurement. A pull-down menu is displayed, listing the available measurement units. Select the display units desired by clicking on the corresponding menu entry. For this test case, change the *Temperature* to Celsius and the *Energy Release Rate* to kilowatts.

4.3.1 Entering Title for the Input File

TITLE: ▮▮▮▮▮▮▮▮▮▮▮▮▮▮▮▮▮▮▮▮▮▮ Before beginning to define the structure, it is typically best to start by assigning a title or description to the input file. Tab to the title field or move the mouse cursor to this field and click with the left mouse button. Enter the text "62 Watts St. Fire" as a title for this example.

4.3.2 Defining Ambient Conditions

To edit the internal and external ambient temperature, pressure, and station elevation along with information on external wind, Tab or move the mouse to the ambient conditions icon in the environment section of the fire scenario overview window, and click or press Enter. For this example, change the internal ambient temperature to 20 °C and the external ambient temperature to 10 °C. Click on *OK* to accept these values and close the Ambient Conditions window.

4.3.3 Specifying Simulation Time and Spreadsheet Output

To specify the simulation time, display time, or output to spreadsheet file with output interval, Tab or move the mouse to the filename icon in the environment section of the fire scenario overview window, and click or press Enter. For this example, enter 3000 s for the simulation time, 10 s for the display interval, 30 s for the spreadsheet interval, and WATTS.TXT for the name of the spreadsheet file.

 Save the file by selecting the diskette icon and select the *Save As* option. Enter the file name as watts.dat and click on *OK* to save the file.

4.3.4 Modifying Compartment Geometry

 In order to model a fire scenario, the user must portray the geometry of the structure in terms of the size and elevation of every compartment in the structure. Thermophysical properties of the enclosing surfaces must also be specified by selecting surface materials in order to accurately model the transfer of heat through the surfaces. When the new data file was defined, default values for the compartment size, surface materials, and vent sizes were defined. These must be customized to fit each specific example. For this example, begin with the fire compartment by selecting the compartment and then the geometry icon to display the geometry window. Modify the compartment sizes as follows: the depth to 6.1 m, the width to 12.8 m, and the interior height to 2.53 m. The enclosing surfaces default to gypsum for the ceiling and walls and plywood for the floor. For this example, only the floor needs to be changed – selecting HARDWOOD from the pull-down list to the right of the floor edit widget. In a similar manner, modify the geometry for compartment (the stairway) as follows: the depth to 3.05 m, the width to 1.22 m, the height to 9.14 m, and the floor surface to HARDWOOD. Click on *OK* to accept these values and close the Geometry window.

 Save the file by selecting the diskette icon and select the *Save* option.

4.3.5 Modifying the Vent Connections

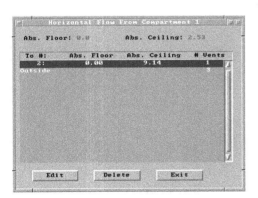 To specify a horizontal flow opening, select the corresponding compartment in the structure graphics list on the fire scenario overview window. When the new data file was defined, several vents were included – doors between the two compartments and the outside, and typical leakages to the outside. These must be customized to fit each specific example. Begin by selecting the fire compartment and Tab or move the mouse to the horizontal flow icon, and click or press Enter. The vent connection window is displayed. Three default vents are shown. Begin by selecting the connections to compartment 2 and select Edit to change the vents to the stairway. For this example, simulate the closed apartment door by changing the soffit height to 0.000213 m – a tiny crack at the bottom of the doorway. This vent

will be modified during the simulation to account for the doorway opened by the firefighters at 2248 s. Click on *OK* to accept these values and close the edit window.

In a similar manner, edit the vents to the outside. Two vents to the outside are displayed in the Horizontal Flow window. For this example, it will be assumed that the apartment was tightly sealed to eliminate air infiltration. The only vent to the outside from the apartment will be assumed to be the working chimney in the living room. Select Outside and the Edit to display the existing vents to the outside. Press *Alt-D* to delete the first predefined vent. The last vent will by customized to simulate the fireplace opening. For this opening, define the width to be 1.321 m, the sill to be 1.1 m, and the soffit to be 1.143 m. Click on *OK* to accept these values and close the edit window. Click on *OK* again to close the vent connection window and return to the fire scenario overview window.

In a similar manner, define two vents from the stairway (compartment 2) to the outside. The exterior door at the bottom of the stairway is 0.91 m wide by 2.13 m high will a sill height of 0.0 m. To simulate the roof vent, a vent is placed near the ceiling with a cross sectional area of 0.84 m^2. Define this vent to be 3.05 m wide with a soffit height of 9.10 m and a sill height of 8.869 m.

 Save the file by selecting the diskette icon and select the *Save* option.

4.3.6 Modifying the Fire Definition

 A medium "t-squared" fire appropriate for this example was defined earlier. To finish the definition, the fire must be customized to position the fire and add the burning trash bags as the first item ignited. The fire position will be modified first. Select the fire icon to display the main fire specification window. For this example, change the fire position to an X position of 2.15 m and a Y position of 1.65 m to approximate the position of the kitchen stove in the apartment. Click on *OK* to accept these values and close the main fire specification window.

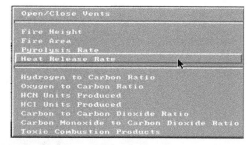 To modify the heat release rate curve for the fire to include the burning trash bags, select the fire compartment from the fire scenario overview window and the time curve icon. Select heat release rate from the menu to display the heat release rate window. Customize the heat release rate curve for this example by including the heat release rate of the burning trash bags as follows: Change the heat release rate for the first two time points (t=0 s and t=500 s) to 25 kW. Click on *OK* to accept these values and return to the fire scenario overview window.

This completes the definition of the test case.

4.3.7 Saving Data File Modifications

 Before the simulation can be run, the user must request the input editor to store the information on the computer's hard disk. All information for the current session of the input editor is grouped together on the hard disk and assigned a unique name referred to as the filename for retrieval purposes in the future. For this example, tab or move the mouse to the diskette icon and select the *Save* option.

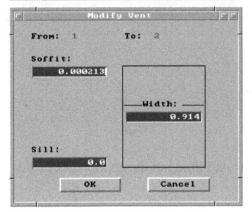

4.4 Running the Simulation

To run the simulation, use the mouse to select the *Run Simulation* icon.

Before beginning the simulation, a window is displayed to provide the user with the option to stop the simulation at a time relative to the beginning of the simulation or to the operation of a detection device. For this example, enter a pause time of 2250 s so that the doorway between the apartment and stairway can be opened. Click on *OK* to accept these inputs and begin the simulation.

When the simulation is paused 2250 s, select *Modify* to display a window which allow the characteristics of the vents to be modified. Select the first entry in the list – the now closed doorway from the apartment to the stairway. Open the doorway by changing the soffit height to 2.13 m. Select *OK* then *Continue* to continue running the simulation.

4.5 Results of the Simulation

The spreadsheet output of the simulation, shown in the window to the right, was used to produce the graph shown below. From the spreadsheet data, an analysis of the simulation can be made.

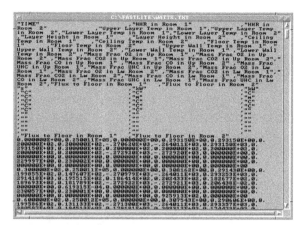

The fire grew briefly to nearly 1 MW over 5 minutes of simulation time, then rapidly throttled back as the oxygen concentration dropped below 10 percent. Temperatures in the apartment peaked briefly at about 300 °C at the time of peak burning, then rapidly dropped below 100 °C as the burning rate fell. The concentration of carbon monoxide (CO) rose to about 3000 ppm and unburned fuel accumulated within the apartment volume during this stage of vitiated combustion.

The front door was opened at about 2250 seconds into the simulation as an estimate of when the first floor team made entry. Immediately, there was an outflow of warm (100 °C) air from the upper part of the doorway, followed by an inrush of ambient air in the lower part of the doorway, followed by the emergence of a large door flame – exactly as reported by the firefighters. This door flame grew within a few seconds to a peak burning rate of more than 5 MW, raising the temperature in the stairway to over 1200 °C – sufficient to melt the glass in the skylight, as observed. Most importantly, the quantity of unburned fuel accumulated in the apartment caused the door flame to persist for more than 7 minutes.

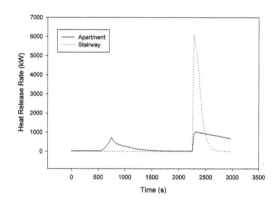

The FAST calculations showed that the theory of the development of this fire was technically sound. The calculations supported the hypothesis that unburned fuel and CO accumulated in an apartment with an open fireplace flue but otherwise tightly sealed, resulting in a backdraft on opening of the apartment door. They showed that sufficient fuel could accumulate under these under ventilated conditions to cause the door flame to persist for the extended period observed. Reported conditions such as flows observed in the doorway, melting of the glass skylight, and fire damage in the apartment and stairway, were consistent with the model results.

5 Estimation Tools

 Quick estimation tools derived from FIREFORM are available in the FAST GUI shell using one of two selection options. Select the *Tools* entry from the desktop menu, or select a compartment on the fire scenario overview window, and click on the tools icon. An input specification window for the selected calculation is displayed. If the calculation tool was selected using the tools icon on the fire scenario overview window, default values are obtained from current input specifications. If the calculation tool was selected from the desktop menu, no default values are available, and the user is required to supply all details. Procedures are discussed in detail in the following subsections. Users unfamiliar with the concepts of a Graphical User Interface (GUI) are strongly encouraged to review these concepts in the Getting Started section of this guide before continuing with the Estimation Tool section. Familiarity with GUI terminology and the use of a mouse is assumed throughout the remainder of this section.

For comparison purposes, the original FIREFORM which accompanied FPETOOL version 3.2 is available from the desktop menu.

The following discussion assumes strict SI units. However, actual data input is dependent upon the measurement units selected by the user.

5.1 Egress Time

This procedure estimates the time needed for a person or group of people to exit an area. The egress movement may be vertical or horizontal and include the use of doorways, stairs, ramps, and corridors. Elevator transportation is not considered.

Theory The egress time calculation assumes that evacuees will travel at user-designated speeds on flat and vertical pathways. These speeds will be altered if the user designates a reduced travel efficiency for the slowest person in the evacuating population. The default travel speed on flat pathways is 76.2 m/min (250 ft/min). The default travel speed on stairs is 12.2 m/min (40 ft/min). Travel time on vertical pathways may be further altered by deviations in standard-stair design measurements. The assumed standard-stair design measurement is a tread depth of 280 mm (11 in.) and a riser height of 178 mm (7 in.). The base speed on stairs is increased for several user-defined parameters. These parameters are increased tread depth, decreased riser height and increased effective width [48] of the stairway. The assumed exitway flow rate is 60 persons/min/$m_{W\text{-effective}}$ (18.3 persons/min/$ft_{W\text{-effective}}$). The rate of travel through enclosed exitways is limited by the flowrate through the doors or door-leaves in the enclosure opening. The doorway calculations assume a default movement rate of one person per second per door-leaf. The standard door-leaf width is 0.76 m (30 in.).

In the equations below, eq (1) represents the time needed for one individual to complete unimpeded egress. Equations (2) - (4) support eq (1). Equation (5) represents the time to move the entire building population through the exterior exit doors. Equation (6) represents the time to move the entire building population through and out of the stairway enclosures. In eq (6) the limit to flow is the $W_{effective}$. The $W_{effective}$ may be either the stairway enclosure exit door width or it could be the width of the stairway itself (protruding handrails or other projections).

$$t_{unimpeded} = \frac{(t_{horizontal} + t_{vertical})}{\chi_{mobility}} \tag{1}$$

$$\chi_{mobility} = \frac{X}{100} \tag{2}$$

Together, eqs (1), (5) and (6) provide a first-order estimate of area evacuation times; the user, however, should be aware of assumptions in arriving at the results. The egress estimates assume the most efficient exit paths are chosen. The procedure does not account for investigation, verification, "way-finding," or assistance. Flow is assumed to proceed ideally and without congestion. There are no adjustments to flow speed in response to evacuee flow density. In light of these inefficiencies, it would be reasonable to expect evacuation times to be two to three times greater than the nominal evacuation time [49]. The nominal evacuation time varies. If any evacuation time from eqs (1), (5) or (6) was an order-of-magnitude greater than the other two evacuation times, then this would be the nominal evacuation time estimate. If the unimpeded evacuation time, ($t_{unimpeded}$) is close to one or both estimates of eqs (5) or (6), then $t_{unimpeded}$ plus a fraction of eqs (5) or (6) is the nominal evacuation time. Conversely, if eqs (5) or (6) exceeds $t_{unimpeded}$, then the nominal evacuation time is the time in eqs (5) or (6) plus a fraction of $t_{unimpeded}$. To determine what value these fractions should be, it is necessary to conduct a more detailed analysis of the evacuation flow [49].

$$t_{horizontal} = \frac{X_{horizontal}}{v_{able}} \tag{3}$$

$$t_{vertical} = \frac{z_{vertical}}{v_{stair}} \sqrt{\frac{11}{7} \frac{z_{riser}}{x_{tread}}} \tag{4}$$

$$t_{exit-opening} = \frac{N_{people}}{N_{exit leaves}} (\frac{exit leaf \cdot sec}{1 \ person}) \tag{5}$$

$$t_{stair} = \frac{N_{people}}{W_{effective}} \frac{1}{\dot{Q}_{stair}} \tag{6}$$

$N_{exit\ leaves}$ Total number of door leaves from the building to the outside

N_{people} Total evacuating population

Q_{stair} People flow rate in a stairway enclosure (default 60 people/min/m $_{W,\ eff}$)

t Exit time (sec)

$W_{effective}$ Effective width of an exit passageway (see Section 3.6.3) (m)

$x_{horizontal}$ Total horizontal distance traversed by the evacuee (m)

v_{able} Speed of an able evacuee moving on flat, dry surface (m/s)

v_{stair} Speed of an able evacuee moving in a vertical means of egress (m/s)

x_{tread} Depth of the tread from riser to riser (m)

X Speed of the slowest evacuee as a percentage of able evacuee speed

z_{riser} Height of the riser from tread to tread (m)

$z_{vertical}$ Total vertical traverse distance (not distance along a sloped incline) (m)

Notes Door leaves less than 5/6 of a standard-door width (0.76 m) should not be considered as an additional leaf available for evacuee egress movement.

Flow rates through door leaves are assumed at one person per second per door leaf. If the door leaf is less than 0.86m (34 in.) then the flow rate may be less. The exitway flow rate is user adjustable. For exit openings substantially larger than 0.86m (34 in.) per door leaf, the flow rate can exceed one person per second. To reflect this potential the user should modify the parameter "Flow rate per door leaf."

Effective flow width for stairs measures wall-to-wall, minus projection of artifacts, minus a clearance distance from the artifacts. This clearance distance is artifact dependent [3]. Typical stairwell effective width is 0.305 m (1 ft) less than actual width. This accounts for the 0.076 m (3 in.) projection of each handrail plus 0.076 m clearance for each handrail.

Turnstiles can have flow rates 1/3 of values for stairwell doorways (20 people/min/m$_{W,\ effective}$).

Stair flow rate is roughly 60 persons per minute per meter of effective width (18.3 persons/min/ft). This flow rate is user adjustable.

If there is more than one stairway and these widths differ, an average width is needed to represent these egress paths because only one stairway width may be entered to this routine. This average width may be calculated such that when multiplied by the number of stairways, it yields a net width equal to the sum of the individual stairway widths.

Emergency travel speed on flat, dry, uncongested surfaces is 76 m/min (250 ft/min). The flow rate is user adjustable; one application follows:

The Americans with Disabilities Act [50] suggest flow rates of 28 m/min (90 ft/min) for disabled evacuees. This represents a speed 37 percent of that assumed for an able person. However, after every 30.5 m (100 ft) of travel, the ADA further suggests that the evacuee will pause for 2 minutes, presumably to rest.

The output parameter "Time required to pass persons through the (building) exit doors..." predicts the waiting time the **last** person in line will experience when completing one of the last parts of their egress path--that of moving from inside to outside of the building. The rate of movement through the exterior-access doors is a function of the number and effective width of these doors. The building population is equally distributed among the specified exterior-access exit doors. A wait during this part of the egress can be caused by insufficient exit doors, inadequate door widths, or a larger-than-anticipated building population.

The output parameter "Time required to pass persons through the stairwell exit doors..." is calculated analogous to "Time required to pass persons through the (building) exit doors..."

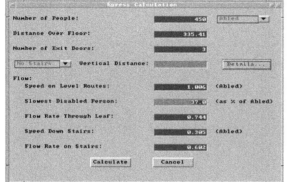

Execution Select *Tools* from the desktop menu or click on the tools icon. Select *Egress Time* from the tools menu. The egress time window is displayed.

Note the display of range and measurement units at the bottom of the window as each edit widget is made the focus widget. To customize the units see the Advanced Features section 6.2.

Number of People: Total number of evacuees using the evacuation routes. Evacuees may be considered "abled" or disabled which modifies the movement speed by the "Slowest Disabled Person" input below.

Distance Over Floor: Total travel distance over level surfaces.

Number of Exit Doors: Total number of exit doors leaves available to evacuees. This number is an integer. To obtain results reflecting additional exit width beyond 0.86m (34 in.) adjust the parameter pertaining to "Flow Rate Through Leaf."

Vertical Distance: Vertical distance moved via stairwell travel. This is not the same as the distance

moved along the slope of a stairway but the vertical distance between the starting and the stopping locations. Note that this input is only available if stairs are selected by the pulldown widget. Additional details of the stairway calculation can be input by selecting *Details...* The number of separate stairways, width of stairways (average or total width), riser height, and tread depth may be input.

Speed on Level Routes: Travel speed of able evacuees over level surfaces.

Slowest Disabled Person: Travel speed of the slowest disabled evacuee expressed as a percentage of the travel speed of able evacuees.

Flow Rate Through Leaf: Travel speed of evacuees through exit doorways, expressed as persons per unit time per exit door leaf.

Speed Down Stairs: Travel speed of able evacuees on stairways.

Flow Rate on Stairs: Flow rate of evacuees on stairways expressed as persons per unit time per unit width of stairway.

Press the *Calculate* button to begin calculation. Upon completion, a results windows is displayed. The "horizontal and stair travel time" is the time estimated for a person to traverse all stair and horizontal paths exclusive of any queuing. Doorways are assumed open and no other evacuees are considered to impede travel rates. The "time required to pass persons through the (building) exit doors" is the time for the entire building population to pass through the available building exit doors. The "time required to pass persons through the stairway exit doors" is the time for the entire building population to pass through the available building stairwell exit doors.

5.2 Sprinkler / Detector Activation

This procedure calculates the thermal response of a detector or sprinkler located at or near a ceiling whose area is large enough to neglect the effects of smoke layer development.

Theory The equations in this procedure were originally distributed in a program written by Evans and Stroup [51] entitled DETACT-QS. The correlations for jet temperatures and velocities were developed from data by Alpert [52]. The theory and documentation for sprinkler activation are presented by Evans [53].

$$T_{D,t+\Delta t} = T_{D,t} + (T_{jet_{t+\Delta t}} - T_{D,t})(1 - e^{-\frac{1}{\tau}}) + (T_{jet_{t+\Delta t}} - T_{jet_t})\tau(e^{-\frac{1}{\tau}} + \frac{1}{\tau} - 1) \qquad (1)$$

The results of this procedure predict time of thermal detector activation. In order to make this prediction, time-dependent events from the fire must be linked to events resulting in the heating of the detector from ambient to its activation temperature. The heat source is accounted for by a user-specified, time varying-fire. The time-lag associated with heating the detector is accounted for with the RTI parameter, eq (2). The RTI parameter considers the detector's ability to absorb heat and the ambient environment's ability to provide heating. Ambient environmental heating is modeled with only forced convection. The temperature and velocity of the convecting air, eqs (3) - (4), are correlations assembled from experimental data of full-scale steady-state and growing fires [52]. The actual heat release rate of the fire should be used with both radiative and convective fractions. When $T_{D,t+\Delta t}$ equals or exceeds the value in $T_{D,\,activation}$, then detector response is predicted.

$$\tau = \frac{RTI}{\sqrt{v_{jet_t}}} \qquad (2)$$

$$v_{jet_t} = 0.95\left(\frac{\dot{q}}{z}\right)^{\frac{1}{3}}, \quad for \quad \frac{r}{z} \leq 0.15$$

$$= 0.2\,\frac{\dot{q}^{\frac{1}{3}}z^{\frac{1}{2}}}{r^{\frac{5}{6}}}, \quad for \quad \frac{r}{z} > 0.15 \tag{3}$$

$$T_{jet_t} = T_\infty + \frac{16.9\,\dot{q}^{\frac{2}{3}}}{z^{\frac{5}{3}}}, \quad for \quad \frac{r}{z} \leq 0.18$$

$$= T_\infty + \frac{5.38}{z}\left(\frac{\dot{q}}{r}\right)^{\frac{2}{3}}, \quad for \quad \frac{r}{z} > 0.18 \tag{4}$$

$\dot{q}$ Total theoretical fire heat release rate

r Radial distance of the sprinkler from the vertical axis of the fire

RTI   Response Time Index: $(mc_p)_{detector}/(hA)\cdot v^{\frac{1}{2}}_{jet}$, a characterization of the detector's thermal sensitivity; a measure of how quickly a detector link reaches its activation temperature.

$T_{jet,t+\Delta t}$ Temperature of the jet at the next time step, $t+\Delta t$

$T_{jet,t}$ Same as $T_{jet,t+\Delta t}$, but at the previous time step, t

T_∞ Ambient space and initial sprinkler temperature

$T_{D,t}$ Detector or link temperature at time, t

$v_{jet,t}$ Velocity of the ceiling jet gases as a function of the parameters on the right-hand side of eqs (2) and (3) at time step, t

z Vertical entrainment distance; the difference between the height of the ceiling and the base of the flames

Notes The total theoretical heat release rate should describe the fire in this correlation [52], [54]. The total theoretical heat release rate may be obtained by multiplying the mass pyrolysis rate by the theoretical heat of combustion. Mass pyrolysis rates can be obtained through experimental measurement using load cells or by analogy with previously burned exemplars. Theoretical heats of combustion are available from handbooks.

The program assumes a quasi-steady-state fire and ceiling jet behavior. This assumption limits the accuracy most when the fire heat release rate changes very rapidly.

The procedure assumes an unconfined ceiling jet and plume. If a smoke layer should develop under the ceiling (as is the case when the fire is large relative to the room), the fire model within FASTLite will consider entrainment of hot gases into the fire plume whereas this procedure will not.

If the detector is located significantly below the bottom of the ceiling jet, then this procedure should not be used. The ceiling jet thickness is estimated between 6 - 12% of the entrainment height (z).

The procedure assumes the detector is located such that it is exposed to both the maximum ceiling jet velocity and temperature.

Correlations for ceiling jet temperature and velocity were determined from limited experimental data: (no beam or truss ceilings, no cathedral ceilings, only smooth, horizontal unconfined ceilings).

Sprinklers or heat detectors located on a wall or on a ceiling next to a wall may have activation times significantly later than predicted activation times. This delay is due to the dissipation of ceiling jet velocity at the wall and wall/ceiling intersection. The dissipation effect may be especially true in room corners.

Rate-of-rise heat detectors are not simulated, only fixed-temperature detectors are simulated.

Radiation and conduction are not accounted for explicitly, but because these phenomena participated in the correlational experiments--to the degree that simulated fire conditions reproduce experimental fire conditions--the radiation/conduction effects are implicitly accounted for. The experimental fire conditions involved wet-pipe sprinklers exposed to cotton, wood, polyurethane, polyvinyl chloride, and liquid heptane fires [51], [55].

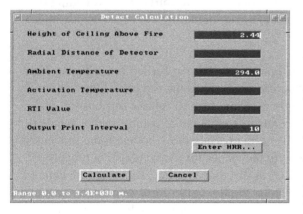

Execution Select *Tools* from the desktop menu or click on the tools icon. Select *Detector/Sprinkler Activation* from the tools menu. The detect calculation window is displayed.

Note the display of range and measurement units at the bottom of the window as each edit widget is made the focus widget. To customize the units see the Advanced Features section 6.2.

Height of Ceiling Above Fire: The difference between the elevation of the lowest point of the fire that can freely entrain air and the elevation of the ceiling.

Radial Distance of Detector: Horizontal distance of the detector location from a vertical axis running through the center of the fire

Ambient Temperature: T_∞, Ambient and initial sprinkler temperature

89

Activation Temperature: $T_{D, activation}$, Detector link activation temperature

RTI Value: Detector response time index. For sprinklers, this is now often given in the manufacturer's catalog. For fixed-temperature heat detectors, The table 1 provides values for devices which correspond to UL spacings. For rate-of-rise detectors, table 2 gives RTI values for three rate-of rise settings (note that 15 °F is typical for U.S. commercial devices).

Output Print Interval: Time interval between hard copy output of time, heat release rate, ceiling jet temperature, and sprinkler / detector link temperature.

Enter HRR...: The heat release rate of the fire as a function of time is entered in a manner similar to the fire for the fire model. Using the mouse, click on the *Enter HRR...* button. The fire curve window is displayed. Note the display of range and measurement units at the bottom of the window as each cell in the edit list widget is made the focus widget. To customize the units see the Advanced Features section 6.2.

If the calculation was selected from the fire scenario window, heat release rate information for the fire is displayed. If no other time-dependent curves have been defined previously for this input file, no entries will be displayed in the spreadsheet. To enter heat release rate time curves for the first time, Tab to the spreadsheet or click on the first cell using the mouse. Enter the actual time at which each fire property is evaluated. Use the vertical scroll bar to enter additional entries beyond those initially displayed. Refer to the GUI Terminology section 1.3.2 of this reference guide for an explanation of the use of scroll bars in the GUI interface.

Movement between time cells is handled using the ↑ and ↓ keys . To insert a new time entry between two existing rows, press Alt-I. To delete a row, press Alt-d. Deleting a row moves all rows following the deleted row up one row. If the entry is to be erased, but all other rows are to remain in current positions, press Alt-e to erase the row. Time entry value ranges are constrained by the entries in surrounding time cells so that time entries within a column of the spreadsheet are ever increasing values. The maximum value allowed is 86400 seconds.

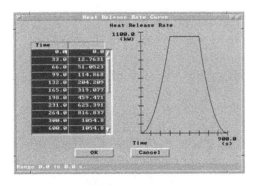

Once the time points have been specified in the first column of the curve spreadsheet, select the top cell of the right column to begin entering the heat release rate curve. Keyboard movement from the time column can be handled using the Shift-→ and pressing the ↑ key until the first cell is reached. Specify the values for the combustion property according to details discussed below. As values are entered in the right column, the fire curve corresponding to time and y-axis entries is plotted on the graph to the right of the spreadsheet.

Table 1. RTI values for fixed temperature heat detectors. RTI values shown are in $(ft\text{-}s)^{1/2}$ / $(m\text{-}s)^{1/2}$. Since the original work was in English units, SI units are approximate.

UL Listed Spacing	UL Listed Activation Temperature						All FM Listed Temps.
	128°F	135°F	145°F	160°F	170°F	196°F	
10/3.1	894/494	738/408	586/324	436/241	358/198	217/120	436/241
15/4.6	559/309	425/235	349/193	246/136	199/110	101/56	246/136
20/6.1	369/204	302/167	235/130	158/87	116/64	38/21	157/87
25/7.1	277/153	224/124	174/75	107/59	72/40	---	107/59
30/9.2	212/117	179/99	136/75	81/45	49/27	---	81/45
40/12.2	159/88	128/71	92/51	40/22	---	---	---
50/15.3	132/73	98/54	67/37	---	---	---	---
70/21.4	81/45	54/30	20/11	---	---	---	---

Note: These RTI's are based on an analysis of the Underwriters Laboratories and Factory Mutual listing test procedures. Plunge test results on the detector to be used will give a more accurate response time index.

Table 2. RTI values for rate-of-rise heat detectors. RTI values shown are in $(ft\text{-}s)^{1/2}$ / $(m\text{-}s)^{1/2}$. Since the original work was in English units, SI units are approximate.

UL Listed Spacing	UL Listed Activation Rate of Temperature Rise		
(ft/m)	15°F/min / 8°C/min	20°F/min / 11°C/min	25°F/min / 14°C/min
10/3.1	1834/1013	1308/722	984/543
12.5/3.8	1453/802	1073/593	805/445
15/4.6	1185/654	872/482	637/352
20/6.1	872/482	581/321	425/235
30/9.2	559/309	380/210	280/155
40/12.2	447/247	291/161	206/114
50/15.3	425/235	246/136	161/89

5.3 Atrium Smoke Temperature

This procedure estimates the average temperature in the smoke layer developing from a fire within an atrium or other large space.

Theory The atrium smoke temperature is derived from the **ASETBX** plume equation [56] that had its own origins from Zukoski [57]. Given an entrainment height and a fire heat release rate, the procedure determines the maximum temperature in the plume.

$$T_{atria} = \frac{220}{1 + 39.8 \left(\dfrac{z^{5/3}}{\dot{q}^{2/3}} \right)} \tag{1}$$

T_{atria}	Temperature rise in atria hot gas layer (°C)
$\dot{q}$	Fire heat release rate (kW)
z	Elevation between lowest point of entrainment and height of interest (m)

Notes The plume theory used in this routine does not apply to the case where plume gases expand to the point of contact with the compartment walls [58]. To ensure that the plume does not touch the wall in the modeled case, the following restriction may be reviewed. The restriction assumes a plume expansion angle of 15° from the vertical.

$$H_{room} \leq \frac{W_{room}}{2 \cdot \sin 15°}$$

Wall heat losses should be negligible. To ensure modeled wall heat-losses are negligible, either the plume should not touch the walls, or the smoke layer should have a temperature below 105 °C (220 °F). Cooper [58] suggests an upper limit on the fire heat release rate (kW) for maintaining moderate wall heat loss. The variable z is defined in eq (1). At fire sizes larger than Q_{limit}, heat from the gases lost to the walls can produce temperatures cooler than predicted.

$$\dot{Q}_{limit} = 333 \, z^{5/2}$$

The heat release rate is steady-state.

The fire is assumed to be a point-source; i.e. no line fires.

The program does not accurately model small fires and/or short entrainment heights.

Execution Select the compartment to be modeled from the fire scenario overview window, or select *Tools* from the desktop menu. If a compartment is selected from the fire scenario overview window, click on the tools icon. Select *Atrium Smoke Temperature* from the tools menu. The following window is displayed:

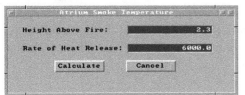

Note the display of range and measurement units at the bottom of the window as each edit widget is made the focus widget. To customize the units see the Advanced Features section 6.2.

Height Above Fire: Entrainment distance from the point where entrainment begins, usually the base of the flames, to the elevation of interest. If this procedure is selected for a compartment on the fire scenario overview window, a height corresponding to the ceiling of the selected compartment is provided as a default value.

Rate of Heat Release: Fire heat release rate.

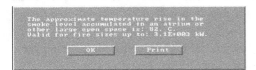

Press the *Calculate* button to begin calculation. Upon completion, a results window is displayed. The approximate plume temperature rise at the user specified height is reported. In addition, the largest actual fire heat release rate that can be used with this correlation for valid temperature approximations is provided.

5.4 Buoyant Gas Head

This procedure calculates the pressure difference between two laterally adjacent gases of different density. In fire safety applications, these density differences are created by differences in smoke and clean air temperatures, but the density differences could also be due to differences in molecular weights of adjacent gases.

Theory The equation used is directly extracted from the manual *Design of Smoke Control Systems in Buildings* [59]. The ambient, colder gas volume is assumed to be 21 °C (70 °F). The pressure

$$\Delta P = 3460 \left(\frac{1}{294} - \frac{1}{T_h} \right) z \tag{1}$$

differential is calculated between the adjacent gases at an elevation coincident with the base of the least dense gas volume.

ΔP Pressure difference between the cold and warm gas (Pa)
T_h Temperature of the hotter gas (K)
z   Thickness of the least dense (hot) gas volume (m)

Notes Conditions are steady-state. Temperature in the hotter, least dense, gas layer is uniform throughout, and the height of the hotter gas volume is constant.

There are no mechanical ventilation/pressurization connections with the hot layer.

Air is the surrounding fluid with a density of 1.2 kg/m³ (0.075 lb/ft³) at 21 °C. Use of this formula in environments where the surrounding gas has a molecular weight or pressure substantially different than a warm-gas layer of air at standard pressure will result in errors.

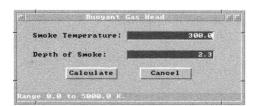

Execution Select the compartment to be modeled from the fire scenario overview window, or select *Tools* from the desktop menu. If a compartment is selected from the fire scenario overview window, click on the tools icon. Select *Buoyant Gas Head* from the tools menu.

Note the display of range and measurement units at the bottom of the window as each edit widget is made the focus widget. To customize the units see the Advanced Features section 6.2.

Smoke Temperature: Temperature of the hot, least dense, layer of gas. If this procedure is selected for a compartment on the fire scenario overview window, the previously specified internal ambient temperature is provided as a default value.

Depth of Smoke: Thickness of the warm air layer.

Press the *Calculate* button to begin calculation. Upon completion, a results window is displayed.

Pressure difference at the base of the hotter gas volume is reported.

5.5 Ceiling Jet Temperature

With this procedure's estimate of ceiling jet temperature one can determine the likelihood of ignition or heat-induced damage at locations *outside* the plume impingement zone.

Theory The likelihood of igniting ceiling combustibles may be determined from ceiling jet temperature estimates provided by this routine [60]. Gas jet temperatures are estimated for radial locations outside the plume impingement zone on the ceiling. The plume impingement radius is 0.2 of the plume clear

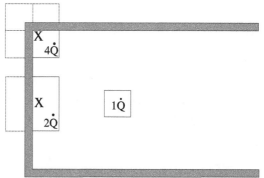

Method of reflection for fires in corners & against walls

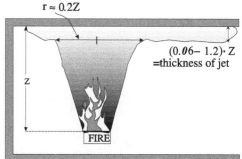

Characteristics of fire plume & ceiling jet

Fire plume and jet characteristics.

entrainment height. The procedure will adjust the temperature of the gas to recognize the changed entrainment characteristics of wall- or corner-positioned fires. The entrainment adjustment is per the method of reflection [61] (12). The procedure also recognizes that any hot gas layer development beneath the ceiling will create an underestimate bias in the temperature predictions. As a precaution to this bias, the procedure approximates the time when this hot layer development will become influential [62].

$$T = T_\infty + 6.81 \frac{(\frac{K\dot{Q}}{r})^{\frac{2}{3}}}{z} \; ; \quad for \; \frac{r}{z} > 0.2 \tag{1}$$

$$t = \frac{20.3 \; A_{ceiling}}{\dot{Q}^{\frac{1}{3}} z^{\frac{2}{3}}} \tag{2}$$

A	Area (m²)
D	Fire diameter (m)
K	Entrainment factor (1 for axisymmetric, 2 for wall-fire, 4 for corner fire)
Q	Total theoretical fire heat release rate (kW)
r	Radial distance from center of the fire to point of interest outside the plume (m)
z	Vertical distance between ceiling and lowest point of the burning fuel (m)
t	Time (second)
T	Jet temperature at height, z, and radial distance, r, from the fire (°C)
T_∞	Ambient temperature (°C)

Notes The total theoretical, not the actual, heat release rate should be used to describe the fire in this and other ceiling/plume correlations by Alpert. The total theoretical heat release rate may be obtained by multiplying the mass pyrolysis rate by the theoretical heat of combustion. Mass pyrolysis rates can be obtained through experimental measurement using load cells. Theoretical heats of combustion are available from handbooks. This fire specification is documented per Alpert's work.

Points considered for examination should be at radial distances greater than 0.2 times the entrainment height from the vertical axis of the fire.

The entrainment height is the vertical distance between the ceiling and the lowest elevation where flaming combustion occurs.

The fire heat release rate is assumed to be steady state. The test fires used in developing the correlation were buoyancy dominated diffusion flames arising from various fuels: wood cribs and pool fires of liquid heptane and ethanol. This procedure is not intended for momentum-dominated jet fires.

The fire is assumed to be a point source; line fires are not considered.

The plume is considered to be unconfined up to the time of predicted layer development.

The method of reflection is appropriately used when flames are attached to a wall or a corner. When the fire is next to but not against the walls, and flames are not touching the wall surfaces, then the reduction in entrainment was not significant [3].

This routine does not consider combustible wall surfaces.

Standard pressure (101,325 Pa) and normal atmospheric gas concentrations (79% N_2, 21% O_2) exist.

This procedure is valid up to the point of hot gas layer development. The actual time to hot layer development can be less than predicted by eq (1) for values of $z/D_{fire} \gg 1$. In addition, eq (2) does not consider fires against a wall or in a corner. The estimated time to hot layer development is inappropriate in such circumstances.

Alpert developed two correlational predictions for ceiling jet temperatures. One correlation was to be used for predicting detector activation and the other for predicting thermal damage. The temperature predictions intended for detector-activation simulations are lower than the temperature predictions intended for thermal damage simulations.

 **Execution** Select the compartment to be modeled from the fire scenario overview window, or select *Tools* from the desktop menu. If a compartment is selected from the fire scenario overview window, click on the tools icon. Select *Ceiling Jet Temperature* from the tools menu.

Note the display of range and measurement units at the bottom of the window as each edit widget is made the focus widget. To customize the units see the Advanced Features section 6.2.

Position of the Fuel: Select either *No nearby walls*, *Fuel package near a wall*, or *Fuel package in a corner*. Experiments have shown [63] that in order for reflection to apply, the fire flames must **touch** the wall.

Ambient Temperature: Compartment temperature at pre-fire conditions. If this procedure is selected for a compartment on the fire scenario overview window, the internal ambient temperature is provided as a default value.

Rate of Heat Release: Total theoretical fire heat release rate.

Distance From Fuel to Ceiling: Elevation difference between the lowest height where flames exist and where air can freely be entrained into the fire, and the height of the ceiling. If this procedure is selected for a compartment on the fire scenario overview window, a height corresponding to the ceiling of the selected compartment is provided as a default value.

Area of Ceiling: If this procedure is selected for a compartment on the fire scenario overview window, an area corresponding to the product of the compartment depth and width is provided as a default value.

Radial Distance From Fire Axis: Lateral distance across ceiling from a point directly over the fire to the point of interest in the ceiling jet.

Press the *Calculate* button to begin calculation. Upon completion, a results window is displayed.

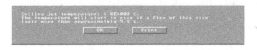

The temperature in the gas jet at specified radial distance and height, and the time when a layer of hot gas that develops under the ceiling can interfere with the "unconfined ceiling jet" assumption are reported.

5.6 Ceiling Plume Temperature

This procedure estimates fire-plume gas temperatures from the height of the continuous flames to the height of the ceiling. This routine complements the *Ceiling Jet Temperature* procedure.

Theory The equation used in this procedure was developed by Alpert and Ward [64] and may be used to estimate the damages caused by the hot plume gases. Figure 12 in *Ceiling Jet Temperature*, section 5.5, illustrates some of the plume geometry variables used in eq (1).

$$T = T_{\infty} + 22.2 \frac{(K \dot{Q}_{fire})^{\frac{2}{3}}}{z^{\frac{5}{3}}} \quad ; \quad for \; \frac{r}{z} \leq 0.2 \tag{1}$$

$$t = \frac{20.3 \, A_{ceiling}}{\dot{Q}^{\frac{1}{3}} z^{\frac{2}{3}}} \tag{2}$$

A	Area (m²)
D_{fire}	Fire diameter (m)
K	Entrainment factor (1 for axisymmetric, 2 for wall-fire, 4 for corner fire)
Q	Total theoretical fire heat release rate (kW)
r	Radial distance from the center of the fire to the point of interest (m)
z	Entrainment height: vertical distance between the ceiling and the lowest point of the burning fuel (m)
t	Time (second)
T	Jet temperature at height, z, and radial distance, r, from the fire (°C)
T_{∞}	Ambient temperature (°C)

Notes The total theoretical, not the actual, heat release rate should be used to describe the fire in this and other ceiling/plume correlations by Alpert [64]. The total theoretical heat release rate may be obtained by multiplying the mass pyrolysis rate with the theoretical heat of combustion. Mass pyrolysis rates can be obtained through experimental measurement using load cells. Theoretical heats of combustion are available from handbooks. This fire specification is documented per Alpert's work.

The heat release rate of the fire is simulated as steady-state. The fire is modeled as a point source; no line fires are considered.

Radial locations from the vertical axis of the fire should be less than 0.2 times the height of the plume.

Radial location should be no further from the vertical axis of the fire than the shortest dimension of the compartment.

Temperature is conservative on the high side compared with experiments used to develop this correlation [64].

The continuous flame height is located at the base of the intermittent flaming region. The temperature of the continuous flaming region is about 800 °C in buoyancy-dominated diffusion flames, but may be as hot as the adiabatic flame temperature under ideal conditions (approximately 1800 °C). The height of the continuous flaming region is below the mean flame height. The mean flame height is defined as the elevation where flames appear 50% of the time [65], [66].

The temperature predictions from wall and corner configurations are theoretical.

The fire must be close enough to a wall that flames touch the surface before the user decides to choose the *Fire near a wall or corner* option. Combustible walls are not considered in this routine.

Standard pressure (101,325 Pa) conditions are used.

Time to hot layer development can be less than predicted for values of $z/D_{fire} \gg 1$.

A hot layer of gas has not developed at the ceiling.

Execution Select the compartment to be modeled from the fire scenario overview window, or select *Tools* from the desktop menu. If a compartment is selected from the fire scenario overview window,

click on the tools icon. Select *Ceiling Plume Temperature* from the tools menu.

Note the display of range and measurement units at the bottom of the window as each edit widget is made the focus widget. To customize the units see the Advanced Features section 6.2.

Position of the Fuel: Select either *No nearby walls*, *Fuel package near a wall*, or *Fuel package in a corner*. Experiments have shown [63] that in order for reflection to apply, the fire flames must **touch** the wall.

Ambient Temperature: Compartment temperature at pre-fire conditions. If this procedure is selected for a compartment on the fire scenario overview window, the internal ambient temperature is provided as a default value.

Rate of Heat Release: Total theoretical fire heat release rate.

Distance From Fuel to Ceiling: Elevation difference between the lowest height where flames exist and where air can freely be entrained into the fire, and the height of the ceiling. If this procedure is selected for a compartment on the fire scenario overview window, a height corresponding to the ceiling of the selected compartment is provided as a default value.

Area of Ceiling: If this procedure is selected for a compartment on the fire scenario overview window, an area corresponding to the product of the compartment depth and width is provided as a default value.

 Press the *Calculate* button to begin calculation. Upon completion, a results window is displayed.

The plume temperature and the time when a layer of hot gas that develops under the ceiling can interfere with the "no layer" assumption are reported.

5.7 Lateral Flame Spread

This procedure estimates the lateral spread of an attached flame along the surface of a thermally thick fuel. "Wind-aided" flame spread is an inappropriate application of this procedure. The procedure is appropriate for flame spread in a direction that is opposite, or normal to, the direction of the propagating flame front.

Theory The equations used in this procedure were developed by Quintiere and Harkelroad [67]. The material properties required by these equations may be experimentally obtained from the Lateral Ignition and Flame spread Test (LIFT) apparatus using procedures outlined in the above reference. The properties include the fuel flame spread parameter (ϕ), the fuel piloted-ignition temperature ($T_{ignition,\ pilot}$), and the fuel thermal inertia ($k\rho c_v$).

The equation for lateral flame spread appears in eq (1). The piloted-ignition temperature for many fuels is quite similar, as the software reference provided with this routine demonstrates.

$$v_{flame,\ lateral} = \frac{\phi}{k\rho c_v} \cdot \frac{1}{(T_{ig} - T_{surface})^2} \tag{1}$$

$v_{flame,\ lateral}$	Lateral rate of attached flame spread (m/s or ft/s)
ϕ	Ignition factor from flame spread test data (kW²/m³)
$k\rho c_v$	Fuel thermal inertia at flame preheat conditions (kW²·s/(m⁴·K²))
$T_{ignition,\ pilot}$	Piloted fuel ignition temperature (°C or °F)
$T_{surface}$	Unignited, ambient-surface temperature (°C or °F)

99

Notes Because temperature is raised to the second power, its impact on the estimated flame velocity is relatively large.

Thermal inertia ($k\rho c_v$) of the fuel is best measured as a single value and at elevated temperatures that accurately simulate conditions during actual flame spread.

It is strongly recommended that data for ϕ and $k\rho c_v$ be obtained from a single test per the suggestions of Quintiere and Harkelroad.

An inappropriate use of this model is for upward flame spread on a wall where unignited fuel in the "shadow" of the flame sheet receives significant preheating.

Experiments have shown correlation with this procedure for lateral extension on a horizontal fuel surface and downward flame extension on a vertical fuel surface [67], [68].

This procedure may not be appropriate for vertically-oriented fuel surfaces that drip when burning.

Execution Select the compartment to be modeled from the fire scenario overview window, or select *Tools* from the desktop menu.   If a compartment is selected from the fire scenario overview window, click on the tools icon. Select *Lateral Flame Spread* from the tools menu.

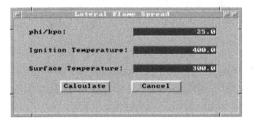

Note the display of range and measurement units at the bottom of the window as each edit widget is made the focus widget. To customize the units see the Advanced Features section 6.2.

phi/kpc: Calculated value of ϕ divided by $k\rho c_v$ for material of interest.

Ignition Temperature: $T_{ignition, pilot}$. If this procedure is selected for a compartment on the fire scenario overview window, the internal ambient temperature is provided as a default value.

Surface Temperature: $T_{surface}$. If this procedure is selected for a compartment on the fire scenario overview window, the internal ambient temperature is provided as a default value.

Press the *Calculate* button to begin calculation. Upon completion, a results window is displayed.

The lateral attached flame spread rate is reported.

5.8 Law's Severity Correlation

This procedure provides a systematic method whereby two fires, one a "real" fire and the other a standard, time-temperature fire, may be compared for equivalence regarding the structural damage imposed by each. Effectively, this procedure answers the question, "Given a known fire, what standard-fire resistance is needed to protect insulated structural members?" The standard, time-temperature fire follows the European specification [69], a close approximation to the ASTM E-119 standard time-temperature curve. The breadth of data from which this correlation was developed [70]. [71] as well as the length of time over which the correlation has been successfully used testifies to its robustness.

Theory The point of comparison between the "real" fire and the "standard" fire is the point in time that a critical temperature is achieved on the surface of a thermally-thick insulated structural element. Law chose 550 °C (1220 °F) as the critical temperature because at this temperature steel's modulus of elasticity or strength is dramatically reduced. However, other critical temperatures could have been chosen just as readily, the net result being a relationship bearing the same form as eq (1) with different constants. It has been demonstrated that other thermally-thick-insulated elements, *e.g.*, concrete and heavy-timber, could be analyzed with this method. Although these other insulated-elements may not fail at the "critical" temperature assumed with this procedure, these elements would nonetheless experience a

$$t_{effective\,resistance} = \frac{m_{fuel}}{\sqrt{A_{vent}A_{room}}} \tag{1}$$

similar surface temperature of approximately 550 °C.

$t_{effective}$ Duration of exposure to the ISO standard time-temperature fire-resistance test that is correlationally equivalent to the "real" fire exposure. (min)

A_{vent} Effective area of all vents. When more than one vent exists, use the method outlined in section 5.13 for calculating an equivalent area. (m²)

A_{room} Area of the compartment surfaces. The calculations *do* include the floor and ceiling area, as well as the area of the walls, less A_{vent}. (m²)

m_{fuel} Mass of dry wood burning in a crib configuration that is equivalent to the total energy released by the "real" fire. (kg)

Notes This procedure requires as input a mass of wood fuel (m_{fuel}) releasing an equivalent energy upon completion of burning as released from complete burning of the "actual" fuel. The mass

$$m_{wood} = \frac{m_{fuel,actual}\Delta H_{c_{fuel,actual}}}{\Delta H_{c_{wood}}} \tag{2}$$

of wood fuel needed as input for the **Fire Load** input parameter described in program execution section may be determined from eq (2). Informed and/or engineering judgement is needed to determine what are appropriate and prudent values for the heats of combustion used in eq (2).

The concept that an exposure time in a standard time-temperature fire can be related to a different exposure time in an actual fire hinges upon the premise that a thermally-protected steel column within each exposure attains the same temperature at the completion of each fire.

101

The correlation assumes the materials providing the estimated fire resistance protection are thermally thick. Thermally thin protection or exposed steel members may not be a valid application for this correlation [70].

The tests used for development of the correlation were conducted in small- and full-scale compartments with concrete and fibre-board insulated walls and a variety of ventilation sizes. Various fuels including tires, liquids, wood cribs, and furniture were used in correlating eq (1) [70,71].

The test configurations all contained open vents. It is recommended that the compartment being investigated possess at least a 0.4 m² (4 ft²) opening. This recommendation is based upon engineering judgement [72].

Execution Select the compartment to be modeled from the fire scenario overview window, or select

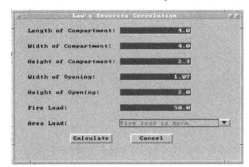

Tools from the desktop menu.   If a compartment is selected from the fire scenario overview window, click on the tools icon. Select *Law's Severity Correlation* from the tools menu. The following window is displayed:

Note the display of range and measurement units at the bottom of the window as each edit widget is made the focus widget. To customize the units see the Advanced Features section 6.2.

Length of the compartment: Depth of the compartment as measured forward from the left, rear corner of the compartment. If this procedure is selected for a compartment on the fire scenario overview window, the depth of the current compartment is displayed as a default value.

Width of the compartment: Width of the compartment as measured across from the left, rear corner of the compartment. If this procedure is selected for a compartment on the fire scenario overview window, the width of the current compartment is provided as a default value.

Height of the compartment: Height of the compartment. If this procedure is selected for a compartment on the fire scenario overview window, the height of the current compartment is provided as a default value.

Width of the opening: Width of the opening or width of an equivalent vent opening calculated from eq (3) in section 5.13 when representing multiple vents in the compartment. If this procedure is selected for a compartment on the fire scenario overview window, the width of a virtual vent that has an area equivalent (for the purposes of determining flashover) to the combined area of all individual vents in the compartment is provided as a default value.

Height of the opening: Height of the opening or height of an equivalent vent opening calculated from eq (3) in section 5.13 when representing multiple vents in the compartment. If this procedure is selected for a compartment on the fire scenario overview window, the height of an equivalent vent using the difference between the elevation of the highest point and the lowest point among all of the vents in the compartment is provided as a default value.

Fire Load: Mass of wood producing a fire equal to the actual fire (kg or lb_m).

Area Load: Toggle selection between *Fire Load is kg/m²* and *Fire Load is gross load*. Selection setting determines units associated with input for the fire load input line.

Press the *Calculate* button to begin calculation. Upon completion, a results window is displayed.

The exposure time in the standard fire test that is equivalent to the time of exposure in a "real" fire is reported.

5.9 Mass Flow Through a Vent

This procedure uses an iterative process to determine an approximate solution for mass flow into and out of a single, naturally-ventilated opening to a compartment containing a steady-state fire. This routine is similar but not identical to the *Smoke Flow Through an Opening* estimation routine.

Theory Conservation of mass is used to solve numerically the gas-mass flow rate into a naturally ventilated compartment with steady-state elevated temperatures, see eq (1).

$$\{Generation\ Rate\} + \dot{m}_{in} - \dot{m}_{out} = \frac{d\,m_{cv}}{dt} \tag{1}$$

$$z_{neutral\ plane} = \frac{1}{1 + \left(\dfrac{T}{T_\infty}\right)^{\frac{1}{3}} \left(1 + \dfrac{\dot{m}_{pyrolysis}}{\dot{m}_{in}}\right)^{\frac{2}{3}}} \tag{2}$$

$$M_o = \frac{\sqrt{\theta}}{1 + \theta} \left(1 - z_{neutral\,plane}\right)^{3/2}, \quad \text{where } \theta = \frac{T - T_\infty}{T_\infty} \tag{3}$$

$$\dot{m}_{out} = \frac{2}{3} C M_o A_{vent} \rho_\infty \sqrt{2g z_{vent}} \tag{4}$$

The mass flow calculation is solved using the conservation of mass principal whereas the smoke flow calculation in section 5.12 is solved using Bernoulli flow and orifice equation assumptions. The solution process begins with the user-specified fuel pyrolysis rate from the "generation rate" term in eq (1). The procedure then estimates a mass inflow rate based upon door width. This inflow rate is used to calculate the neutral-plane elevation ($z_{neutral-plane}$) using eq (2). The neutral plane elevation is subsequently used to calculate the mass outflow rate, see eq (3) and (4). If mass conservation does not close within the specified criteria, then the bisection numerical technique estimates again and the process repeats until convergence or excess iterations are achieved [73]. Some of the first work on these vent flow rates was presented by Kawagoe [74].

In the conservation of mass equation, the pyrolysis rate is a source term, and as such its value is inserted in the generation rate term of eq (1). Since this procedure assumes a steady-state elevated temperature in the compartment, the net rate-of-change in mass within the compartment ($d[m_{cv}]/dt$) is zero.

$\dot{m}_{pyrolysis}$ Mass generation rate of the fuel (g/s)

$\dot{m}_{cv}$ Net mass of gas within the control volume (the control volume is the compartment air-volume not including the wall/ceiling materials).

z_{vent} Height of the vent opening from soffit to sill (m)

$z_{neutral\ plane}$ Height of the neutral plane in the vertical opening of the door (m)

T   Temperature of the hot gas layer (K)

T_∞ Temperature of the ambient, outside air (K)

θ Non-dimensionalized temperature variable $(T - T_\infty)/T_\infty$

Notes Air flows are motivated by buoyancy forces only: no mechanical pressurization, stack effect or wind effects are considered.

Conditions are steady state: pyrolysis rate is constant, layer temperatures are constant, layer heat losses are constant, momentum flow across the vent is constant. Examples of steady-state conditions could be flashover, or fuel controlled burning when the fire is not growing.

The gas in the compartment is either at a uniform temperature, *e.g.*, flashover, or is in a ventilation-limited condition. This procedure is inappropriate for early stages in a fire when a hot layer increases in thickness and the expansion of gases causes only an outflow from the compartment.

There is either one opening in the space, or all of the openings are at approximately the same level in the compartment. If openings must be combined, they should be combined per the method used in Thomas's Flashover Correlation, section 5.13.

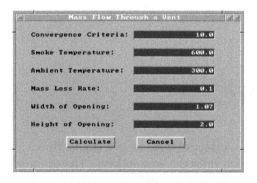

Execution Select the compartment to be modeled from the fire scenario overview window, or select *Tools* from the desktop menu. If a compartment is selected from the fire scenario overview window, click on the tools icon. Select *Mass Flow Through a Vent* from the tools menu.

Note the display of range and measurement units at the bottom of the window as each edit widget is made the focus widget. To customize the units see the Advanced Features section 6.2.

Convergence Criteria: Criterion for numerical solution of eq (2).

Smoke Temperature: Temperature of the hot, upper layer of gas. If this procedure is selected for a compartment on the fire scenario overview window, the previously specified internal ambient temperature is provided as a default value.

Ambient Temperature: Temperature of the ambient, outside temperature. If this procedure is selected for a compartment on the fire scenario overview window, the previously specified external ambient temperature is provided as a default value.

Mass Loss Rate: Fuel pyrolysis rate.

Width of the opening: Width of the opening or width of an equivalent vent opening calculated from eq (3) in section 5.13 when representing multiple vents in the compartment. If this procedure is selected for a compartment on the fire scenario overview window, the width of a virtual vent that has an area equivalent (for the purposes of determining flashover) to the combined area of all individual vents in the compartment is provided as a default value.

Height of the opening: Height of the opening or height of an equivalent vent opening calculated from eq (3) in section 5.13 when representing multiple vents in the compartment. If this procedure is selected for a compartment on the fire scenario overview window, the height of an equivalent vent using the difference between the elevation of the highest point and the lowest point among all of the vents in the compartment is provided as a default value.

Execution: Press the *Calculate* button to begin calculation. Upon completion, a results window is displayed.

The mass flow rates in and out of the compartment are reported. In addition, the absolute height of the neutral plane above the bottom of the vent is displayed. This variable is also expressed as the nondimensionsal height of the neutral plane in the door. Finally, a percentage of vent area filled is calculated and displayed.

5.10 Plume Filling Rate

This procedure estimates the volume flow of smoke and entrained air in a plume at a point above the flames of a fire of constant heat release rate.

Theory There are currently several models [75], [76], [77], [78] that estimate entrainment into a rising buoyant plume. Each model provides roughly the same accuracy with no individual model clearly outperforming the others in all cases. This procedure uses a model originated by Zukoski and later modified by Cooper and Stroup [79].

The equation used by this procedure is:

$$\dot{V}(z) = 0.0026\left(1-\chi_r\right)\dot{Q} + 0.006047\left(\left(1-\chi_r-\chi_o\right)\dot{Q}\right)^{1/3}z^{5/3} \tag{1}$$

$\dot{V}(z)$	Volumetric flow rate of all gases in the plume at height z (Liters/s)
Q	Theoretical fire heat release rate (kW/s)
χ_r	Fraction of Q released through radiative heat transfer
χ_o	Fraction of Q not released via radiative or convective heat into the plume

z   Height in the plume where $\dot{V}(z)$ is calculated (m)

Notes This procedure applies to steady-state fires.

The input parameter χ_o may be used to account for combustion inefficiencies and/or heat from the fire that is expended in pyrolyzing fuel. If χ_o is non-zero, then the sum of χ_o and χ_r should be less than one.

This procedure should not be applied at heights equal to or less than the mean flame height. The mean flame height is that elevation on the central fire axis where flames appear 50% of the time. The mean flame height also correlates with an average gas temperature of 500 °C. [76].

Other plume models have been verified in large atria [80].

The approximate conversion between Liters/s and cubic feet per minute is 2.12. To convert from L/s to cfm, multiply the number representing flow in L/s by 2.12.

The fire is considered a point source; i.e., no line fires or fire areas in a distributed sense are considered.

This procedure does not consider wall or corner fires.

The buoyant gas has no appreciable horizontal momentum.

There is no contact between the walls of the compartment and the plume (mathematically the walls are a distance, r, from the fire: $r \geq 0.2 * H$).

This procedure should not be used on predominantly momentum-driven plumes.

The plume is not tilted from the vertical and the plume is not experiencing wind- or mechanically-aided entrainment.

Execution Select the compartment to be modeled from the fire scenario overview window, or select *Tools* from the desktop menu. If a compartment is selected from the fire scenario overview window, click on the tools icon. Select *Plume Filling Rate* from the tools menu.

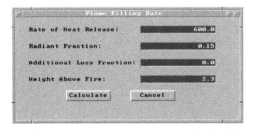

Note the display of range and measurement units at the bottom of the window as each edit widget is made the focus widget. To customize the units see the Advanced Features section 6.2.

Rate of Heat Release: Fire heat release rate.

Radiant Fraction: Fraction of heat distributed via radiative energy [81].

Additional Loss Fraction: Fraction of heat not convected and not radiatively distributed.

Height Above Fire: Elevation difference between the point of interest in the plume and the lowest height where entrainment begins. For diffusion flames this is usually the base of the flames.

Press the *Calculate* button to begin calculation. Upon completion, a results window is displayed.

Volumetric flow rate in the plume at the specified height above the fire is reported.

5.11 Radiant Ignition of a Near Fuel

This is a quick, simplistic estimation method for determining what size fire will radiatively ignite a nearby fuel; no flame impingement is assumed.

Theory The equations in this procedure were obtained through correlation of experimental data [82]. The experiments examined the fire sizes necessary to ignite a second, remote, initially non-burning fuel item that was not in direct contact with the flame or convective flow of the original fire. The experimental data provided a correlation between the peak heat release rate of the first-burning item and the maximum distance to a second non-burning fuel item that would result in ignition. Babrauskas found the second item could usually be categorized into one of three groups--based upon material and size:

- **Easily Ignited** - material ignites when it receives a radiant flux of 10 kW/m² or greater. Examples are thin materials such as curtains or draperies.

$$\dot{Q}_{fire} = 30.0 \times 10^{\left(\frac{Distance\ +\ 0.08}{0.89}\right)} \qquad (1)$$

- **Normally Resistant to Ignition** - material ignites when it receives a radiant flux of 20 kW/m² or greater. Examples are upholstered furniture and other materials with significant mass but small thermal inertia ($k\rho c_p$).

$$\dot{Q}_{fire} = 30\left(\frac{Distance\ +\ 0.05}{0.019}\right) \qquad (2)$$

- **Difficult to Ignite** - material ignites when it receives a radiant flux of 40 kW/m² or greater. Examples are thermoset plastics and other thick materials (greater than 0.013 m [½ in.]) with substantial thermal inertia ($k\rho c_p$).

$$\dot{Q}_{fire} = 30\left(\frac{Distance\ +\ 0.02}{0.0092}\right) \qquad (3)$$

Q_{fire}	Fire heat release rate (kW)
α	Regression coefficient of experimentally measured data (m)
β	Regression coefficient of experimentally measured data (m)

Notes The least accuracy is obtained when analyzing "Easy to ignite" items. This is because the required heat release rates for igniting these types of fuels are low enough that small changes in fuel properties can result in large percentage changes for the required ignition heat release rates.

Target fuels do not have flame impingement considered in the ignition analysis.

The distance between the exposed fuel item and the initial burning fuel is small enough to nullify a point source radiation assumption. The target-fuel item assumedly sees a broad fire such as that produced by a free-standing upholstered chair or side of a couch.

Fuel types included in the experimental correlation were: wood, plywood, plywood laminates, paper, polyurethane and polyethylene. These fuel types have a radiative fraction varying from 0.6 for polyurethane to 0.3 for wood pine [83].

Execution Select the compartment to be modeled from the fire scenario overview window, or select *Tools* from the desktop menu.   If a compartment is selected from the fire scenario overview window, click on the tools icon. Select *Radiant Ignition* from the tools menu.

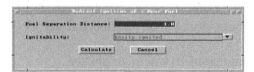

Note the display of range and measurement units at the bottom of the window as each edit widget is made the focus widget. To customize the units see the Advanced Features section 6.2.

Fuel Separation Distance: Separation of fuel packages.

Ignitability: Select either *Easily Ignited*, *Normally Resistant to Ignition*, or *Difficult to Ignite*. For easily ignitable fuels, the energy flux is 10 kW/m². For normal fuels, the energy flux is 20 Kw/m², and for difficult to ignite fuels, the energy flux is 40 kW/m².

Press the *Calculate* button to begin calculation. Upon completion, a results window is displayed.

The fire size of the initially burning fuel needed to ignite the second fuel source is reported.

5.12 Smoke Flow Through an Opening

This procedure estimates the steady-state volumetric flow rate of heated gas at elevated temperatures through an opening in an enclosure. It is appropriate for measuring post-flashover or steady-state smoke leakage through open doors or cracks around closed doors. Whereas this procedure solves for the volumetric smoke flow rate at a given temperature, the *Mass Flow Through a Vent* discussed in section 5.13 solves for the vent flow in terms of mass.

Theory The theory for smoke flow through an opening due to buoyancy forces is developed in *Design of Smoke Control Management Systems*, [84]. The derivation foundation is the classical orifice eq (1). In contrast, the mass flow through a vent calculation discussed previously in section 5.13 iterates on a solution satisfying mass conservation. The velocity term in eq (1) may be substituted for by rearranging the Bernoulli expression, eq (2), and solving for velocity in terms of the other parameters, eq (2b). The assumptions for Bernoulli flow are presented in the following notes section. The pressure term in eq (2b) is solved by rearranging the ideal gas law, see eq (3), and expressing pressure in terms of gas density.

$$\dot{V} = CA_{vent}v \tag{1}$$

$$\frac{\Delta P_1}{\rho_1} + \frac{v_1^2}{2} + gz_1 = \frac{\Delta P_2}{\rho_2} + \frac{v_2^2}{2} + gz_2 \tag{2}$$

$$v_2 = \sqrt{\frac{\Delta P_{(1-2)}}{\rho_2}} \tag{2b}$$

$$\Delta P_{1-2} = \Delta \rho_{1-2} gh \tag{3}$$

$$\Delta \rho_{1-2} = \frac{P(MW)}{R} \left| \frac{1}{T_1} - \frac{1}{T_2} \right| \tag{3b}$$

$$\dot{V} = CA_{vent} \sqrt{\frac{2ghP(MW)}{\rho_2 R} \left| \frac{1}{T_1} - \frac{1}{T_2} \right|} \tag{4}$$

A_{vent}	Area of the vent that allows smoke movement (m²)
C	Orifice coefficient (0.8)
g	Acceleration constant equal to Earth's surface gravity (9.81 m/s²)
h	Height of the neutral plane (m)
MW	Ambient fluid molecular weight ($28.95 \cdot 10^{-3}$ kg air/(g·mole))
P	Standard pressure (101,325 Pa)
ΔP_{1-2}	Pressure difference across the vent (Pa)
R	Universal gas constant (8.314 J/((g·mole)·K)))
T	Air temperature (K)
T_∞	Ambient air temperature (294 K)
$\dot{V}$	Volumetric vent flow rate (m³/s)
z	Elevation difference (m)
v	Smoke velocity (m/s)
$\Delta \rho_{1-2}$	Density difference across the vent (kg/m³)

Subscript

1	Location inside the compartment
2	Location just beyond the vent

Notes Assumes uniform depth of smoke in the vent area.

Steady-state flow conditions are assumed.

Bernoulli fluid is steady-state, incompressible, and nonviscous.

Only buoyancy driven smoke flow is considered.

Standard pressure, no stack effect, no air-handling systems, no wind forces, no unrelieved pressure-volume work by the expanding, hot smoke.

Standard gravitational acceleration at Earth's surface, *i.e.*, smoke flow is not considered in systems undergoing additional accelerations. The heated smoke layer is quiescent away from the vent.

Inappropriate for duct-like openings where the passage length is significantly greater than the narrow dimension of the opening.

Air is the ambient gas (or any other ambient gas having a similar molecular weight) at a temperature of 21 °C (70 °F).

The temperature should characterize the average conditions throughout the smoke layer.

Execution Select the compartment to be modeled from the fire scenario overview window, or select *Tools* from the desktop menu.   If a compartment is selected from the fire scenario overview window, click on the tools icon. Select *Smoke Flow Through an Opening* from the tools menu.

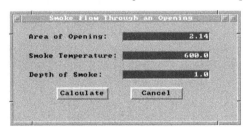

Note the display of range and measurement units at the bottom of the window as each edit widget is made the focus widget. To customize the units see the Advanced Features section 6.2.

Area of Opening: Area of the opening or area of an equivalent vent opening calculated from eq (3) in section 5.13 when representing multiple vents in the compartment. If this procedure is selected for a compartment on the fire scenario overview window, the area of a virtual vent as discussed in the Thomas's Flashover Correlation is provided as a default value.

Smoke Temperature: Temperature of the hot, upper layer of gas. If this procedure is selected for a compartment on the fire scenario overview window, the previously specified internal ambient temperature is provided as a default value.

Depth of Smoke: Depth of the smoke layer.

Press the *Calculate* button to begin calculation. Upon completion, a results window is displayed.

The volumetric smoke flow rate out of the vent area is reported.

5.13 Thomas's Flashover Correlation

This procedure quickly estimates the amount of energy needed to produce flashover in a compartment.

Theory This procedure [85] results from simplifications applied to a hot-layer energy balance on a compartment with a fire. These simplifications resulted in eq (1). The first term represents heat losses to the "...total internal surface area of the compartment...", and the second term represents energy flow out of the vent opening. The two constants in eq (1) represent values correlated to experimental flashover conditions.

$$\dot{Q} = 7.8 A_{room} + 378 \left(A_{vent} \sqrt{H_{vent}} \right)_{equivalent} \tag{1}$$

$$A_{room} = A_{floor} + A_{ceiling} + A_{walls} - A_{vents_{equivalent}} \tag{2}$$

$$A_{vents_{equivalent}} = H_{vent_{equivalent}} \cdot W_{vent_{equivalent}} \tag{3}$$

$$W_{vent_{equivalent}} = \frac{\left(A_{vent} \sqrt{H_{vent}} \right)_1 + \left(A_{vent} \sqrt{H_{vent}} \right)_2 + \dots}{H^{\frac{3}{2}}_{vent_{equivalent}}} \tag{4}$$

Q =   Fire heat release rate (kW)

A_{vent} =   Area of the vent (m²)

$H_{vent, equivalent}$ =   The difference between the elevation of the highest point among all of the vents and the lowest point among all of the vents (m).

$W_{vent, equivalent}$ =   The width of a virtual vent that has an area equivalent (for the purposes of determining flashover) to the combined area of all individual vents from the compartment of consideration (m).

Notes The formulation of the energy balance considered heat losses from the hot gas layer and heated walls to the cooler lower walls and floor surfaces. The term A_{room} should include all surfaces inside the compartment, exclusive of the vent area.

The fire area should not be subtracted from the floor area as the fire will conduct and convect heat into the floor underneath the fuel footprint.

The equation does not know where the vent is located, nor whether the vent is a window or a door; however, the equation was developed from tests that included window venting.

The equation does not consider whether the walls are insulated or not. Use of the equation for compartments with thin metal walls may therefore be inappropriate. The experiments included compartments with thermally thick walls and fires of wood cribs. The equation was later verified in gypsum lined compartments with furniture fires [86].

Verification with fast growing fires: the correlation was developed from fast not slow growing fires.

This procedure was correlated from experiments conducted in compartments not exceeding 16 m² in floor area.

The equation predicts flashover in spaces without ventilation. This prediction is unlikely due to oxygen starvation of the fire.

Execution Select the compartment to be modeled from the fire scenario overview window, or select *Tools* from the desktop menu.   If a compartment is selected from the fire scenario overview window, click on the tools icon. Select *Thomas Flashover* from the tools menu.

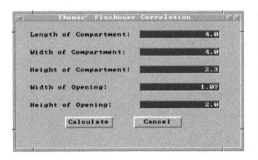

Note the display of range and measurement units at the bottom of the window as each edit widget is made the focus widget. To customize the units see the Advanced Features section 6.2.

Length of the compartment: Depth of the compartment as measured forward from the left, rear corner of the compartment. If this procedure is selected for a compartment on the fire scenario overview window, the depth of the current compartment is displayed as a default value.

Width of the compartment: Width of the compartment as measured across from the left, rear corner of the compartment. If this procedure is selected for a compartment on the fire scenario overview window, the width of the current compartment is provided as a default value.

Height of the compartment: Height of the compartment. If this procedure is selected for a compartment on the fire scenario overview window, the height of the current compartment is provided as a default value.

Width of the opening: Width of the opening or width of an equivalent vent opening calculated from eq (3) when representing multiple vents in the compartment. If this procedure is selected for a compartment on the fire scenario overview window, the width of a virtual vent that has an area equivalent (for the purposes of determining flashover) to the combined area of all individual vents in the compartment is provided as a default value.

Height of the opening: Height of the opening or height of an equivalent vent opening calculated from eq (3) when representing multiple vents in the compartment. If this procedure is selected for a compartment on the fire scenario overview window, the height of an equivalent vent using the difference between the elevation of the highest point and the lowest point among all of the vents in the compartment is provided as a default value.

Press the *Calculate* button to begin calculation. Upon
completion, a results window is displayed.

The estimated fire heat release rate that will create flashover
is displayed. In addition, the estimated energy losses from gas flow out of the door and from the gas to
compartment wall surfaces are reported.

5.14 Ventilation Limit

This procedure estimates the maximum post-flashover fire size sustainable in a compartment based upon
the ventilation geometry. Vent geometry can control the fire size by limiting the amount of air entering
the compartment and hence limiting the amount of oxygen that may combine with the fuel.

Theory Kawagoe [87] originally presented the idea that fire heat release rate within a compartment
could be limited by ventilation geometry. This idea was borne out by Kawagoe's original--and many
subsequent post-flashover experiments (for example, [88], [89]). The equation implemented in this
procedure is presented in eq (1) where the mass flow rate of air into the compartment $\frac{1}{2}A_o H_o^{\frac{1}{2}}$ is in kg/s.

$$\dot{Q}_{VL} = \chi_A \Delta H_{c,air} \frac{1}{2} A_o \sqrt{H_o} \qquad (1)$$

Q_{VL}	Limit of fire heat release rate supportable by a naturally ventilated compartment (kW)
χ_A	Combustion efficiency
A_o	Area of the opening (m²)
H_o	Height of opening (m)
$\Delta h_{c,air}$	Fuel heat of combustion per kilogram of air that oxidizes fuel (~3000 kJ/kg).

Notes It is possible to calculate the dimensions of a single vent that will sustain the fire burning rate
allowed by several individual vents each contributing air (oxidizer) to the fire up to the limit supported
by their geometrical size. The dimensions of this equivalent vent are obtainable from eq (3) in section
5.13. If the ventilation limit procedure is selected for an existing compartment in the input editor, the
equivalent vent dimensions for that compartment are provided as default inputs.

The equivalent vent dimension approach is not appropriate for use when vents are located at significantly
different elevations in the wall.

This routine is not applicable to the early times in the growth of a compartment fire when fuel-limited
burning occurs. In this situation, more than enough air needed to sustain burning passes through the vent
and reaches the fuel.

This routine will calculate the heat released inside the compartment; however, it is possible that
additional heat may be released outside of the compartment that is unaccounted for by this procedure.
This can occur if during ventilation limited burning, the fire pyrolyzes more fuel than the air is capable of
burning. The unburned pyrolyzate will be carried out the vent and may burn in a "door or window jet"

providing that the pyrolyzate concentrations are high enough, hot enough, and sufficient oxygen for combustion is present.

Assuming χ_A as unity results in a prediction for the largest possible ventilation limit fire; this may be appropriate for design fires used in life-safety hazard analysis.

Execution Select the compartment to be modeled from the fire scenario overview window, or select *Tools* from the desktop menu. If a compartment is selected from the fire scenario overview window,

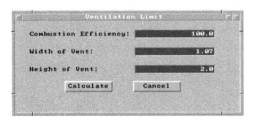

click on the tools icon. Select *Ventilation Limit* from the tools menu displayed.

Note the display of range and measurement units at the bottom of the window as each edit widget is made the focus widget. To customize the units see the Advanced Features section 6.2.

Combustion efficiency: For combustion efficiency, refer to reference below.

Width of vent: Width of the vent or width of an equivalent vent calculated from eq (3) in section 5.13 when representing multiple vents in the compartment. If this procedure is selected for a compartment on the fire scenario overview window, the width of a virtual vent that has an area equivalent (for the purposes of determining flashover) to the combined area of all individual vents in the compartment is provided as a default value.

Height of vent: Height of the vent or height of an equivalent vent calculated from eq (3) in section 5.13 when representing multiple vents in the compartment. If this procedure is selected for a compartment on the fire scenario overview window, the height of an equivalent vent using the difference between the elevation of the highest point and the lowest point among all of the vents in the compartment is provided as a default value.

Press the *Calculate* button to begin calculation. Upon completion, a results window is displayed.

The Fire heat release rate as limited by ventilation geometry is reported.

6 Utilities

Users unfamiliar with the concepts of a Graphical User Interface (GUI) are strongly encouraged to review these concepts in the Getting Started section of this guide before continuing with the Utilities section. Familiarity with GUI terminology and the use of a mouse is assumed throughout the remainder of this section.

6.1 Changing Directories

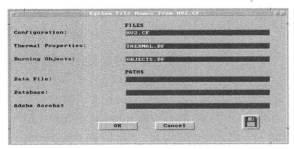

FAST supports the use of file directory structures to enable the user to store input information and databases by projects or other user specific groupings. A new installation of the FAST software stores all files in the directory from which the software is started. Users can customize the directory structures to appropriately reflect the environment in which they work by selecting *Options* from the desktop menu then selecting *File Names*.

Directory names are entered in the lower section of the input window under the *PATHS* heading. Next to the *Data Files* label, enter the directory from which input data to the fire model is to be obtained. Directory names can use absolute path referencing including drive and path names, or relative addressing from the startup directory of the FAST software. Next to the *Database* label, enter the directory from which the model is to obtain the thermophysical and objects database details.

If the specified directories are to be used only for the current FAST software run, click on the *OK* button and continue with input in the GUI shell.

If the specified directories are to be used every time the FAST software is run, click on the disk icon in the lower right corner of the window. This saves current settings to the configuration file indicated in the first edit widget of the window.

6.2 Changing Display Units

As the user enters information for edit widgets within the GUI shell, range messages for the current widget are displayed at the bottom of each input window along with the user selected measurement units. A new installation of the FAST software displays measurements in standard SI units. Users can customize the display measurement units to appropriately reflect the environment in which they work by selecting *Options* from the desktop menu then selecting *User Specified Units*.

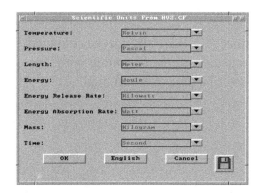

Modifications are made to a set of eight (8) base measurements from which all other measurements within the GUI shell are derived. These eight measurements include: temperature, pressure, length, energy, energy release rate, energy absorption rate, mass, and time. Assuming that the installation selections are in place, SI measurement display unit settings for each of these measurements are: temperature - K, pressure - Pa, energy - J, energy release rate - W, energy absorption rate - W, mass - kg, and time - s. With these base measurement settings, the display units for some derived measurements are: specific heat - J/kg*K, mass loss rate - kg/s, and volumetric rate change - m^3/s. To modify the settings for any of the base measurements, click on the pull-down icon to the right of the measurement.

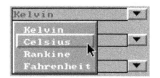

A pull-down menu is displayed, listing the available measurement units. Select the display units desired by clicking on the corresponding menu entry.

It is important to remember that modifications made are reflected in all measurements derived from the selected base measurement. For example, if units for length are changed from meters to feet, area references in the GUI shell will indicate ft^2, volume will indicate ft^3, and velocity will indicate ft/s.

To modify the default SI setting to use English units, click on the center text button at the bottom of the window. Units for all base measurements are set to standard English values. The text displayed on this button is dependent on the current setting of the base measurements. If current units are SI, the text *English* is displayed. If current units are English, the text *Metric* is displayed.

If the selected units are to be used only for the current FAST software run, click on the *OK* button and continue with input in the GUI shell.

 If the selected units are to be used every time the FAST software is run, click on the disk icon in the lower right corner of the window. This saves current settings to the configuration file indicated in the first edit widget.

6.3 Customizing Colors and Patterns

Some support is provided to allow the user to customize the desktop and window colors and patterns to suit individual preferences. At the current time, colors used for widgets such as the white on blue edit widgets, or the white on cyan message line, cannot be modified by the user. Select *Options* from the desktop menu then select *Display*.

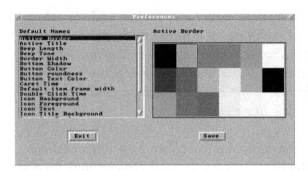

The selection list on the left allows the user to select the item to be modified. Although many attributes of the GUI interface can be modified through this window, the user is encouraged to restrict modifications to colors and patterns only. Some of the attribute modifications are not applicable to the DOS environment, but could impact FAST installations in the future. Typically, the following attributes can be modified:

Active Border (color) - color of the rectangular frame around the outside of the focus window
Active Title (color) - color of the title bar on the focus window
Inactive Border (color) - color of the rectangular frame around the outside of non-focus windows
Inactive Title (color) - color of the title bar on non-focus windows
Inactive Title Text (color) - color of the text in the title bar on non-focus windows
Screen Background (color) - color of the desktop background
Screen Background (pattern) - pattern of the desktop background
Scrollbar (color) - color of scrollbars on the focus window
Title Text (color) - color of the text in the title bar on the focus window
Window Background (color) - color of the window

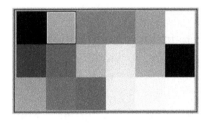

To modify any of these attributes, select the entry from the selection list on the left. Display on the right of the window reflects the options for the selection made by the user. If user selection involves modifying a color, a color list is displayed.

Click on the color desired.

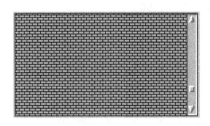

If selection involves modifying a pattern, a pattern selection list is displayed.

Scroll the list until a desirable pattern is displayed.

117

Once all attributes have been modified, click on the *Save* button to save the customized user preferences. Modifications to window attributes are reflected in the current session. Modifications to the desktop attributes require the user to exit the FAST software and restart.

6.4 Input Editor Error Log

As input files are read, and the overview windows in the input editor are created, a file of errors encountered in the input file is generated by the FAST software. If critical errors are

encountered, a red message window is displayed prior to displaying the fire scenario overview window. To view the list of errors, select *Utilities* from the desktop menu, then select *View Errors*.

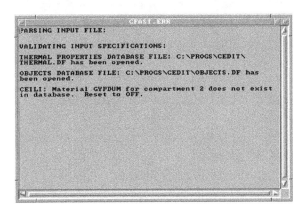

Use the vertical scroll bar to view other sections of the file. Refer to the GUI Terminology section 1.3.2 of this reference guide for an explanation of the use of scroll bars in the GUI interface.

In the top left corner of the window, a horizontal bar is displayed inside a small square. To close the window, position the mouse pointer on this line and double-click.

6.5 Copy File

FAST supports a copy file utility to enable the user to copy one input file, database file, configuration file, or other ASCII text file to another file name prior to making modifications. To copy a file, select *Utilities* from the desktop menu, then select *Copy File*. A window is displayed.

Copy From: Enter the full filename including path and directory to be copied. If a partial

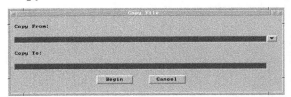

filename is known, enter the known characters along with * to indicate those parts of the filename for which characters are not known, press the pull-down icon. If the pull-down icon is pressed, the file name window is displayed.

The file specification window consists of four key elements: the filename edit widget, the directory edit widget, the directory selection list, and the filename selection list. To search

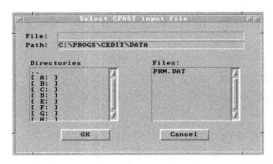

directories other than the current directory displayed in the directory edit widget, enter the new directory name in the directory edit widget and press Enter. Directories may also be selected by double-clicking on the drive or directory in the directory selection list. If the filename is known, enter it in the filename edit widget and press Enter. Do not include the drive or directory in the filename. Drive and directory specifications are handled only through the directory edit widget and the directory selection list widget. Once the desired file is found, double-click on the entry in the filename selection list, or single-click and press the *OK* button.

Copy To: Enter the full filename including path and directory where the file is to be copied. If the specified file already exists, a warning message is displayed requesting confirmation before overwriting the file.

Press *Begin* to begin copying the file, or *Cancel* to exit this procedure without copying the file.

6.6 Print File

FAST supports a print file utility to enable the user to print an input file or other ASCII text file through a selected printer port. To print a file, select *Utilities* from the desktop menu, then select

Print File. The print file window is displayed.

Print From: Enter the full filename including path and directory to be printed. If a partial filename is known, enter the known characters along with * to indicate those parts of the filename for which characters are not known, press the pull-down icon. If the pull-down icon is pressed, the file name window is displayed:

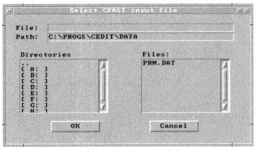

The file specification window consists of four key elements: the filename edit widget, the directory edit widget, the directory selection list, and the filename selection list. To search directories other than the current directory displayed in the directory edit widget, enter the new directory name in the directory edit widget and press Enter. Directories may also be selected by double-clicking on the drive or directory in the directory selection list. If the filename is known, enter it in the filename edit widget and press Enter. Do not include the drive or directory in the filename. Drive and directory specifications are handled only through the directory edit widget and the directory selection list widget. Once the desired file is found, double-click on the entry in the filename selection list, or single-click and press the *OK* button.

Print To: Selections include: *lpt1*, *lpt2*, *com1*, *com2*, *com3*, and *com4*. If the specified port is not available, a warning message is displayed requesting confirmation prior to printing the file.

Press *Begin* to begin printing the file, or *Cancel* to exit this procedure without printing the file.

6.7 View File

FAST supports a view file utility to enable the user to view an input file, configuration file, or other ASCII text file. To view a file, select *Utilities* from the desktop menu, then select *View File*. The view file window is displayed.

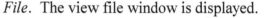

View File: Enter the full filename including path and directory to be viewed. If a partial filename is known, enter the known characters along with * to indicate those parts of the filename for which characters are not known, press the pull-down icon. If the pull-down icon is pressed, the following window is displayed:

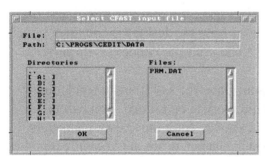

The file specification window consists of four key elements: the filename edit widget, the directory edit widget, the directory selection list, and the filename selection list. To search directories other than the current directory displayed in the directory edit widget, enter the new directory name in the directory edit widget and press Enter. Directories may also be selected by double-clicking on the drive or directory in the directory selection list. If the filename is known, enter it in the filename edit widget and press Enter. Do not include the drive or directory in the filename. Drive and directory specifications are handled only through the directory edit widget and the directory selection list widget. Once the desired file is found, double-click on the entry in the filename selection list, or single-click and press the *OK* button.

Press *Begin* to begin viewing the file, or *Cancel* to exit this procedure without viewing the file.

Use the vertical scroll bar to view other sections of the file. Refer to the GUI Terminology section 1.3.2 of this reference guide for an explanation of the use of scroll bars in the GUI interface.

 In the top left corner of the window, a horizontal bar is displayed inside a small square. To close the window, position the mouse pointer on this line and double-click.

6.8 Delete File

FAST supports a delete file utility to enable the user to delete an input file, configuration file, or

other ASCII text file. To delete a file, select *Utilities* from the desktop menu, then select *Delete File*. The delete file window is displayed.

Delete File: Enter the full filename including path and directory to be deleted. If a partial filename is known, enter the known characters along with * to indicate those parts of the filename for which characters are not known, press the pull-down icon. If the pull-down icon is pressed, the file name window is displayed.

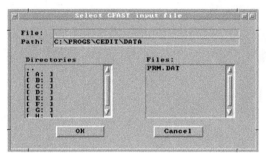

The file specification window consists of four key elements: the filename edit widget, the directory edit widget, the directory selection list, and the filename selection list. To search directories other than the current directory displayed in the directory edit widget, enter the new directory name in the directory edit widget and press Enter. Directories may also be selected by double-clicking on the drive or directory in the directory selection list. If the filename is known, enter it in the filename edit widget and press Enter. Do not include the drive or directory in the filename. Drive and directory specifications are handled only through the directory edit widget and the directory selection list widget. Once the desired file is found, double-click on the entry in the filename selection list, or single-click and press the *OK* button.

Press *Begin* to begin deleting the file, or *Cancel* to exit this procedure without deleting the file.

7 References

[1]   Bukowski, R.W., "Strawman Procedure for Assessing Toxic Hazard." In Summary preliminary report of the advisory committee on the toxicity of the products of combustion. NFPA, Quincy, MA; June 1984.

[2]   Lawson, J.R. and Quintiere, J.G., "Slide-rule Estimates of Fire Growth," Natl. Bur. Stand. (U.S.), NBSIR 85-3196, Gaithersburg, MD, pp. 56. (1985).

[3]   Nelson, H.E., "FIREFORM: A Computerized Collection of Convenient Fire Safety Computations," Natl. Bur. Stand. (U.S.), NBSIR 86-3308 (1986).

[4]   Bukowski, R. W., Peacock, R. D., Jones, W. W., and Forney, C. L., "Technical reference guide for the HAZARD I fire hazard assessment method," Handbook 146 Volume II, Natl. Inst. Stand. Technol. (June 1989).

[5]   Bukowski, R. W., Peacock, R. D., Jones, W. W., and Forney, C. L., "Software user's guide for the HAZARD I fire hazard assessment method," Handbook 146 Volume I, Natl. Inst. Stand. Technol. (June 1989).

[6]   Peacock, R. D., Forney, G. P., Reneke, P. A., Portier, R. W., and Jones, W. W., "CFAST, the Consolidated Model of Fire Growth and Smoke Transport," Natl. Inst. Stand. Technol, Technical Note 1299, 241 pp (1993).

[7]   Portier, R. W., Peacock, R. D., and Reneke, P. A., "FASTLite: Engineering Tools for Estimating Fire Growth and Smoke Transports," Natl. Inst. Stand. Technol., Special Pub. 899, 86 pp (1996).

[8]   Friedman, R., "Survey of Computer Models for Fire and Smoke," Factory Mutual Research Corp., Norwood, MA, 02062 1990.

[9]   Cooper, L.Y., "A Mathematical Model for Estimating Available Safe Egress Time in Fires," Fire and Materials. 1982, *6(4)*, 135-144.

[10]   Babrauskas, V., "COMPF2-A Program for Calculating Post-Flashover Fire Temperatures," Natl. Bur. Stand. (U.S.) 1979, Tech. Note 991, 76 p.

[11]   Davis, W. D. and Cooper, L. Y., "Computer Model for Estimating the Response of Sprinkler Links to Compartment Fires With Draft Curtains and Fusible Link-Actuated Ceiling Vents," Fire Technology 1991, *27 (2)*, 113-127.

[12]   Mitler, H.E. and Emmons, H.W., "Documentation for CFCV, the Fifth Harvard Computer Fire Code," Nat. Bur. Stand. (U.S.) 1981, NBSGCR 81-344, 187 p.

[13]   Mitler, H. E. and Rockett, J., "A User's Guide for FIRST, a Comprehensive Single Room Fire Model," Natl. Bur. Stand. (U. S.) 1987, NBSIR 87-3595.

[14]   Tanaka, T., "A Model of Multiroom Fire Spread," Nat. Bur. Stand. (U.S.) 1983, NBSIR 83-2718, 175 p.

[15]   Gahm, J. B., "Computer Fire Code VI, Volume I," Nat. Bur. Stand. (U.S.) 1983, NBS GCR 83-451, 116 p.

[16]   Jones, W. W., A Multicompartment Model for the Spread of Fire, Smoke and Toxic Gases, Fire Safety Journal 9, 55 (1985); Jones, W. W. and Peacock, R. D., Refinement and Experimental Verification of a Model for Fire Growth and Smoke Transport, Proceedings of the 2nd International Symposium on Fire Safety Science, Tokyo (1989); Jones, W. W. and Peacock, R. D., "Technical Reference Guide for FAST Version 18" Natl. Inst. Stand. Technol. Tech. Note 1262 (1989).

[17]   Forney, G. P. and Cooper, L. Y., The Consolidated Compartment Fire Model (CCFM) Computer Application CCFM.VENTS - Part II: Software Reference Guide, Nat. Inst. Stand. Technol., NISTIR 90-4343 (1990).

[18]   Jones, W. W. and Forney, G. P. "A Programmer's Reference Manual for CFAST, the Unified Model of Fire Growth and Smoke Transport," Natl. Inst. Stand. Technol. 1990, Tech. Note 1283, 104 p.

[19]   Mitler, H. E. "Comparison of Several Compartment Fire Models: An Interim Report," Natl. Bur. Stand. (U.S.) 1985, NBSIR 85-3233, 33 p.

[20]   Jones, W. W. "A Review of Compartment Fire Models," Natl. Bur. Stand. (U.S.) 1983, NBSIR 83-2684, 41 p.

[21]   Deal, S. "A Review of Four Compartment Fires with Four Compartment Fire Models," *Fire Safety Developments and Testing*, Proceedings of the Annual Meeting of the Fire Retardant Chemicals Association. October 21-24, 1990, *Ponte Verde Beach, Florida*, 33-51.

[22]   Peacock, R. D., Jones, W. W., and Bukowski, R. W., "Verification of a Model of Fire and Smoke Transport," Fire Safety J., **21** 89-129 (1993).

[23]   Duong, D. Q., "The Accuracy of Computer Fire Models: Some Comparisons with Experimental Data from Australia," Fire Safety J. 1990, 16(6), 415-431.

[24]   Davis, W. D., Notarianni, K. A., and McGrattan, K. B., "Comparison of Fire Model Predictions with Experiments Conducted in a Hangar with a 15 Meter Ceiling," Natl. Inst. Stand. Technol., NISTIR 5927 (1996).

[25] Babrauskas, V., Lawson, J. R., Walton, W. D., Twilley, W. H., "Upholstered Furniture Heat Release Rates Measured with a Furniture Calorimeter," Natl. Bur. Stand. (U.S.), NBSIR 82-2604, 1982.

[26] Babrauskas, V. and Krasny, J. F., "Fire Behavior of Upholstered Furniture," Natl. Bur. Stand. (U.S.), Monogr. 173, 1985.

[27] Lee, B.T., "Effect of Ventilation on the Rates of Heat, Smoke, and Carbon Monoxide Production in a Typical Jail Cell Fire," Natl. Bur. Stand. (U.S.), NBSIR 82-2469, 1982.

[28] Pitts, W. M, Johnsson, E. L., and Bryner, N. P., "Carbon Monoxide Formation in Fires by High-Temperature Anaerobic Wood Pyrolysis," Combustion Institute. Symposium (International) on Combustion, 25th. Proceedings. July 31-August 5, 1994, Irvine CA, Combustion Institute, Piitsburgh, PA, 1455-1462 (1994).

[29] Pitts, W. M., The Global Equivalence Ratio Concept and the Formation Mechanisms of Carbon Monoxide in Enclosure Fires, Prog. Energy Combust. Sci., **21** 197-237 (1995).

[30] Peacock, R. D., Davis, S., Lee, B. T., "An Experimental Data Set for the Accuracy Assessment of Room Fire Models," Natl. Bur. Stand. (U.S.), NBSIR 88-3752, April 1988, p. 120.

[31] Babrauskas, V., Levin, B.C., Gann, R.G., "A New Approach to Fire Toxicity Data for Hazard Evaluation," ASTM Standardization News, September 1986.

[32] Schifiliti, R. P, Meacham, B. J., and Custer, R. L. P., "Design of Detection Systems," Chapter 4-1 in The SFPE Handbook of Fire Protection Engineering, Second Edition, DiNenno, P.J., et. al., editors, National Fire Protection Association, HFPE-95 (1995).

[33] Heskestad, G. and Delichatsios, M.A., "Environments of Fire Detectors - Phase 1: Effect of Fire Size, Ceiling Height, and Material. Volume 2. Analysis," NBS-GCR-77-95, Natl. Bur. Stand. (U.S.), 100pp (1977).

[34] Stroup, D.W. and Evans, D.D., "Use of Computer Models for Analyzing Thermal Detector Spacing," Fire Safety Journal. **14**, 33-45 (1988).

[35] "Standard for the Installation of Sprinkler Systems," NFPA 13, 1994 Edition, National Fire Protection Association (1994).

[36] Evans, D. D., "Sprinkler Fire Suppression Algorithm for HAZARD," Natl. Inst. Stand. Technol., NISTIR 5254 (1993).

[37] Drysdale, D., "An Introduction to Fire Dynamics," John Wiley and Sons, New York, 143 p. (1985).

[38]   Tewarson, A., "Combustion of Methanol in a Horizontal Pool Configuration," Factory Mutual Research Corp., Norwood, MA, Report No. RC78-TP-55 (1978).

[39]   McCaffrey, B. J., "Entrainment and Heat Flux of Buoyant Diffusion Flames," Natl. Bur. Stand. (U.S.), NBSIR 82-2473, 35 p. (1982).

[40]   Koseki, H., "Combustion Properties of Large Liquid Pool Fires," Fire Technology, **25(3)**, 241-255 (1989).

[41]   Welty, J.R, Wicks, C.E, Wilson, R.E., *Fundamentals of Momentum, Heat and Mass Transfer, 3rd ed.,* John Wiley and Sons, New York, NY, 1984.

[42]   Moody, L.F., "Friction "Factors for Pipe Flow," Transactions of ASME, Vol. 66, 1944, p. 671-684.

[43]   Huebscher, R. G., "Friction Equivalents for Round, Square, and Rectangular Ducts," ASHVE Transactions (renamed ASHRAE Transactions), Vol. 54, pp 101-144.

[44]   Heyt, J. W., and Diaz, J. M., "Pressure Drop in Flat-Oval Spiral Air Duct," ASHRAE Transactions, Col. 81, Part 2, pp 221-230.

[45]   Galloway, F. M., and Hirschler, M. M., "Transport and Decay of Hydrogen Chloride: Use of a Model to Predict Hydrogen Chloride Concentration in Fire Involving a Room-Corridor-Room Arrangement," Fire Safety Journal 16, pp. 33-52, 1990.

[46]   Schifiliti, R. P., "Use of Fire Plume Theory in the Design and Analysis of Fire Detector and Sprinkler Response," Master's Thesis, Worcester Polytechnic Institute, Worcester, MA (1986).

[47]   Lawson, J.R., Walton, W.D., and Twilley, W. H., "Fire Performance of Furnishings as Measured in the NBS Furniture Calorimeter," Natl. Bur. Stand. (U.S.), NBS IR 83-2787 (1984).

[48]   Pauls, J., "Movement of People,"Chapter 3-13 in the SFPE Handbook of Fire Protection Engineering, Second Edition, DiNenno, P.J., et. al., editors, National Fire Protection Association, HFPE-95 (1995).

[49]   Nelson, H.E. and McLennan, H.A., "Emergency Movement," Chapter 3-14 in the SFPE Handbook of Fire Protection Engineering, Second Edition, DiNenno, P.J., et. al., editors, National Fire Protection Association, HFPE-95 (1995).

[50]   U. S. Department of Justice, "Nondiscrimination on the Basis of Disability by Public Accommodations and in Commercial Facilities: American with Disabilities Act, 28 CFR Part 36, Appendix A, Guidelines, A4.3.1 (1), Federal Register, 1991.

[51]   Evans, D. D. and Stroup, D. W., "Methods to Calculate the Response of Heat and Smoke Detectors Installed Below Large Unobstructed Ceilings," Natl. Bur. Stand. (U.S.), NBSIR 85-3167 (1985).

[52]   Alpert, R. L., "Calculation of Response Time of Ceiling-Mounted Fire Detectors," Fire Technology, Vol 8:(3), National Fire Protection Association, Quincy, MA, pp. 181-195 (1972).

[53]   Evans, D. D., "Calculating Fire Plume Characteristics in a Two-Layer Environment," Fire Technology, Vol. 20:(3), National Fire Protection Association, Quincy, MA, pp. 39-63 (1984).

[54]   Alpert, R.L., and Ward, E. J.; "Evaluating Unsprinklered Fire Hazards;" SFPE Technology Report 83-2; Society of Fire Protection Engineers: Boston, MA (1983).

[55]   Heskestad, G. and Delicatsios, M.A., "Environments of Fire Detectors--Phase I. Effect of Fire Size, Ceiling Height and Material," Natl. Bur. Stand. (U.S.), NBS-GCR-77-86 (1977).

[56]   Walton, W. D., "ASET-B, A Room Fire Program for Personal Computers," Natl. Bur. Stand. (U.S.), NBSIR 85-3144 (1985).

[57]   Zukoski, E. E.; "Development of a Stratified Ceiling Layer in the Early Stages of a Closed-Room Fire," Fire and Materials, Vol. 2, No. 2 (1978).

[58]   Cooper, L. Y. and Stroup, D. W., "Calculating Available Safe Egress Time from Fires," Natl. Bur. Stand. (U.S.), NBSIR 82-2587 (1982).

[59]   Klote, J.H. and Milke, J.A., "Design of Smoke Control Management Systems," ASHRAE and SFPE, Atlanta, GA 30329 (1992).

[60]   Alpert, R.L. and Ward, E. J.; "Evaluating Unsprinklered Fire Hazards," SFPE Technology Report 83-2; Society of Fire Protection Engineers: Boston, MA (1983).

[61]   Zukoski, E.E., Kubota, T. and Cetegen, B., "Entrainment in the Near Field of a Fire Plume. Final Report," Natl. Bur. Stand. (U.S.), NBS-GCR-81-346 (1981).

[62]   Nelson, H.E., "FPETOOL: Fire Protection Engineering Tools for Hazard Estimation," Natl. Inst. Stand. Technol., NISTIR 4380 (1990).

[63]   Evans, D., "Ceiling Jet Flows," Chapter 2-4 in the SFPE Handbook of Fire Protection Engineering, Second Edition, DiNenno, P.J., et. al., editors, National Fire Protection Association, HFPE-95 (1995).

[64]   Alpert, R.L. and Ward, E. J.; "Evaluating Unsprinklered Fire Hazards;" SFPE Technology Report 83-2, Society of Fire Protection Engineers: Boston, MA (1983).

[65]   Heskestad, G. "Fire Plumes," Chapter 2-2 in the SFPE Handbook of Fire Protection Engineering, Second Edition, DiNenno, P.J., et. al., editors, National Fire Protection Association, HFPE-95 (1995).

[66]   McCaffrey B.J. "Flame Height," Chapter 2-1 in the SFPE Handbook of Fire Protection Engineering, Second Edition, DiNenno, P.J., et. al., editors, National Fire Protection Association, HFPE-95 (1995).

[67]   Quintiere, J.G. and Harkelroad, M.F., "New Concepts for Measuring Flame Spread Properties," Symposium on Application of Fire Science to Fire Engineering: American Society for Testing and Materials and Society of Fire Protection Engineers, Denver, CO, 27 June 1984.

[68]   Quintiere, J.G., "A Semi-Quantitative Model for the Burning of Solid Materials," Natl. Inst. Stand. Technol., NISTIR 4840 (1992).

[69]   Fire Resistance Tests of Structures, International Organization for Standardization Recommendation R834 (1968).

[70]   Law, M., "Prediction of Fire Resistance," Proceedings, Symposium No. 5, Fire-resistance Requirements for Buildings - A New Approach; Joint Fire Research Organization, London, Her Majesty's Stationery Office (1973).

[71]   Thomas, P.H. and Heseldon, A.J.M., "Fully-developed fires in single compartments. A co-operative research promgramme of the Conseil International du Bâtiment," Joint Fire Research Organization Fire Research Note No. 923 (1972).

[72]   Nelson, H.E., "FPETOOL: Fire Protection Engineering Tools for Hazard Estimation," Natl. Inst. Stand. Technol., NISTIR 4380 (1990).

[73]   Lawson, J.R. and Quintiere, J.G., "Slide-rule Estimates of Fire Growth," Natl. Bur. Stand. (U.S.), NBSIR 85-3196 (1985).

[74]   Kawagoe, K. D. and Sekine, T., "Estimation of Fire Temperature-Time Curve for Rooms," BRI Occasionial Report No. 11, Building Research Institute, Ministry of Construction, Japanese Government (1963).

[75]   McCaffrey, B.J., "Purely Buoyant Diffusion Flames: Some Experimental Results," Combustion Institute: Eastern States Section (1978).

[76]   Zukoski E., "Development of a Stratified Ceiling Layer in the Early Stages of a Closed-Room Fire," Fire and Materials, Vol. 2, No. 2 (1978).

[77]   Morton, B.R., Taylor, G. and Turner, J.S., "Turbulent Gravitational Convection from Maintained and Instantaneous Sources," Proceedings of the Royal Society of London, Series A, No. 1196, London, England (1956).

[78]   Heskestad, G., "Engineering Relations for Fire Plumes," Fire Safety Journal, Vol. 7, pp. 25-32 (1984).

[79]   Cooper, L. Y. and Stroup, D. W., "Calculating Available Safe Egress Time from Fires," Natl. Bur. Stand. (U.S.), NBSIR 82-2587 (1982).

[80]   Grubitts, S. and Shestopal, V.O., "Computer Program for an Uninhibited Smoke Plume and Associated Computer Software," Fire Technology, Vol 29, (3), pp. 246-67 (1993).

[81]   Tewarson, A., "Generation of Heat and Chemical Compounds in Fires," Chapter 3-4 in the SFPE Handbook of Fire Protection Engineering, Second Edition, DiNenno, P.J., et. al., editors, National Fire Protection Association, HFPE-95 (1995).

[82]   Babrauskas, V., "Will the Second Item Ignite," Natl. Bur. Stand. (U.S.), NBSIR 81-2271 (1982).

[83]   Tewarson, A., "Generation of Heat and Chemical Compounds in Fires," Chapter 3-4 in the SFPE Handbook of Fire Protection Engineering, Second Edition, DiNenno, P.J., et. al., editors, National Fire Protection Association, HFPE-95 (1995).

[84]   Klote, J.H. and Milke, J.A., "Design of Smoke Control Management Systems," ASHRAE and SFPE, Atlanta, GA 30329, pp. 21-32 (1992).

[85]   Thomas, P. H., "Testing Products and Materials for Their Contribution to Flashover in Rooms," Fire and Materials, 5, pp. 103-111 (1981).

[86]   Babrauskas, V., "Upholstered Furniture Room Fires--Measurements, Comparison with Furniture Calorimeter Data, and Flashover Predictions," *Journal of Fire Sciences*, Vol. 2, 5 (1984).

[87]   Kawagoe, K. D. and Sekine, T., "Estimation of Fire Temperature-Time Curve for Rooms," BRI Occasionial Report No. 11, Building Research Institute, Ministry of Construction, Japanese Government (1963).

[88]   Fang, J.B. and Breese, J.N., "Fire Development in Residential Basement Rooms, Interim Report," Natl. Bur. Stand. (U.S.), NBSIR 80-2120 (1980).

[89]   Babrauskas, V., "COMPF2--A Program for Calculating Post-Flashover Fire Temperatures," Natl. Bur. Stand. (U.S.), Technical Note 991 (1979).

Appendix A CFAST Input Data File Format

The CFAST model requires a description of the problem to be solved. This section provides a description for the input data used by the model. In general, the order of the data is not important. The one exception to this is the first line which specifies the version number and gives the data file a title.

Most entries in the input data file can be generated using FAST. FAST provides online help information in addition to context-sensitive error checking. For example, FAST will not allow the user to select a fire compartment outside the range of compartments specified on the Geometry screen. Because of these features, FAST is the preferred method for creating and editing most CFAST input files. However, some input file key words are not supported by FAST. For these special cases, editing of the ASCII input file using any ASCII text editor is necessary. The following sections detail the available input file key words and group them by their availability within FAST. Subsection titles for the FAST key words correspond to the subsection titles in the FAST chapter of this reference. This has been done as an aid to understanding the organization of the input file.

The number of lines in a given data set will vary depending, for example, on the number of openings or the number of species tracked. A number of parameters such as heat transfer and flow coefficients have been set within CFAST as constants.

A.1 General Format of an Input File Line

Each line of the data file begins with a key word which identifies the type of data on the line. The key words currently available are listed below. The maximum number of arguments for each keyword is shown in parentheses at the right of the description for the keyword.

ADUMPF	specify a file name for saving time histories in spreadsheet form	(2)
CEILI	specify name of ceiling descriptor(s)	(N)
CFCON	ceiling floor heat conduction	(2)
CHEMI	miscellaneous parameters for kinetics	(7)
CJET	ceiling jet	(1)
CO	CO/CO_2 mass ratio	(lfmax)
CT	fraction of fuel which is toxic	(lfmax)
CVENT	opening/closing parameter	(lfmax + 3)
DEPTH	depth of compartments	(N)
DETECT	fire detection and suppression	(9)
DUMPR	specify a file name for saving time histories	(1)
EAMB	external ambient	(3)

FAREA	area of the base of the fire	(lfmax)
FHIGH	height of the base of the fire	(lfmax)
FLOOR	specify the name of floor property descriptor(s)	(N)
FMASS	pyrolysis rate	(lfmax)
FPOS	exact position of the fire using x, y, z coordinates	(3)
FQDOT	heat release rate	(lfmax)
FTIME	points of time on the fire timeline	(Lfmax + 1)
HALL	specify corridor flow model	(1)
HCL	hcl/pyrolysis mass ratio	(lfmax)
HCN	hcn/pyrolysis mass ratio	(lfmax)
HCR	hydrogen/carbon mass ratio of the fuel	(lfmax)
HEIGH	interior height of a compartment	(N)
HI/F	absolute height of the floor of a compartment	(N)
HVENT	specify vent which connect compartments horizontally	(7)
INELV	specify **interior** node elevations (for ventilation ducts)	(2 x # of interior nodes)
LFBO	compartment of fire origin	(1)
LFBT	type of fire	(1)
LFPOS	position of the fire in the compartment	(1)
MVDCT	describe a piece of (circular) duct work	(9)
MVFAN	give the pressure - flow relationship for a fan	(5 to 9)
MVOPN	Specify an opening between a compartment and ventilation system	(5)
OBJECT	additional objects to be burned	(7)
OBJFL	alternative object database file	(1)
OD	C/CO_2 mass ratio	(lfmax)
O2	ratio of oxygen to carbon in the fuel	(lfmax)
RESTR	specify a restart file	(2)
SELECT	specify compartments for graphical display in GUI interface	(3)
SHAFT	specify single zone model for a compartment	(1)
STPMAX	specify maximum ODE solver timestep	(1)
TAMB	ambient inside the structure	(3)
TARG	specify a simplified wall surface target	
TARGET	specify targets for calculation of local surface temperature and flux	(10)
THRMF	alternative thermal properties file	(1)
TIMES	time step control of the output	(5)
VERSN	version number and title	(fixed format 2)
VVENT	specify a vent which connects compartments vertically	(4)
WALLS	specify the name of wall property descriptor(s)	(N)
WIDTH	width of the compartments	(N)
WIND	scaling rule for wind effects	(3)

The number in parenthesis is the maximum number of entries for that line. "N" represents the number of compartments being modeled. The outside (ambient) is designated by one more than the number of compartments, N+1. Thus, a three compartment model would refer to the outside as compartment four. An entry for lfmax is no longer supported directly. The value for lfmax is determined by the number of entries on the FTIME line.

Each line of input consists of a label followed by one or more alphanumeric parameters associated with that input label. The label must always begin in the first space of the line and be in capital letters. Following the label, the values may start in any column, and all values must be separated by either a comma or a space. Values may contain decimal points if needed or desired. They are not required. Units are standard SI units. Most parameters have default values which can be utilized by omitting the appropriate line. These are indicated in the discussion. The maximum line length is 128 characters, so all data for each key word must fit in this number of characters.

A.2 Entering a Title for the Input File

The first line in the file must be the version identification along with an optional short description for the simulation. It is a required input. The VERSN line is the line that CFAST keys on to determine whether it has a correct data file. The format is fixed, that is the data must appear in the columns specified in the text.

Example:

```
VERSN    1 Example Case for FAST User's Guide
```

Key word: VERSN	
Inputs: Version Number, Title	
Version Number	The version number parameter specifies the version of the CFAST model for which the input data file was prepared. Normally, this would be 3. It must be in columns 8-9.
Title	The title is optional and may consist of letters, numbers, and/or symbols that start in column 11 and may be up to 50 characters. It permits the user to uniquely label each run.

A.3 Specifying Simulation and Output Times

A TIMES line is also required in order to specify the length of time over which the simulation takes place.

133

Example:

```
VERSN     1 Example Case for CFAST 1.6 User's Guide
TIMES     200    10    10    0    0
```

Key word: TIMES Inputs: Simulation time, Print Interval, History Interval, Display Interval, Copy Count	
Simulation Time (s)	Simulation time is the length of time over which the simulation takes place. The maximum value for this input is 86400 s (1 day). The simulation time parameter is required.
Print Interval (s)	The print interval is the time interval between each printing of the output values. If omitted or less than or equal to zero, no printing of the output values will occur.
History Interval (s)	The history interval is the time interval between each writing of the output to the history file. The history file stores all of the output of the model at the specified interval in a format which can be efficiently retrieved for use by other programs. Section A.13 provides details of the history file. A zero must be used if no history file is to be used.
Display Interval (s)	The display interval is the time interval between each graphical display of the output as specified in the graphics specification, section A.16. If omitted, no graphical display will occur. There is a maximum of 900 intervals allowed. If the choice for this parameter would yield more than 900 writes, the graphs are truncated to the first 900 points.
Copy Count	Copy count is the number of copies of each graphical display to be made on the selected hard copy device as specified in the graphics specification, section A.16. If omitted, a value of zero (no copies) is assumed.

When running simulations in the GUI interface, up to three compartments may be selected and displayed in tabular and graphical form as the simulation proceeds. The SELECT keyword specifies the user's choice for the (up to) three compartments.

Key word: SELECT	
Input: Compartment 1, Compartment 2, Compartment 3	
Compartment 1 Compartment 2 Compartment 3	Each of up to three inputs may be included on the input line to specify the compartments to be displayed in tabular, graphical, and spreadsheet form during the simulation. The compartment numbers may be in any order and any compartments included in the simulation may be selected. Entries less than one, or greater than the number of compartments in the simulation are ignored.

Example:

```
SELECT 3 1 2
SELECT 1 0 0
```

There are several files which CFAST uses to communicate with its environment. They include 1) a configuration file, 2) the thermal database, 3) the objects database, 4) a history file, and 5) a restart file. The format of the thermal database and objects database are detailed in Appendices B and C.

The output of the simulation may be written to a disk file for further processing by programs such as REPORT or to restart the CFAST model from the end of a previous simulation. At each interval of time as specified by the history interval in the TIMES label, the output is written to the file specified. For efficient disk storage and optimum speed, the data is stored in an internal format and cannot be read directly with a text editor. The RESTR line is an optional line used to restart the model at a specified simulation time within an existing history file.

Example:

```
DUMPR PRM.HI
ADUMPF PRM.CSV NF
```

Key word: ADUMPF	
Input: Spreadsheet File, Output Options	
Spreadsheet File	The name specifies a file (up to 63 characters) to which the program outputs are written in a form readable by spreadsheet programs. Spreadsheet file is an optional input. If omitted, the file will not be generated. Note that in order to obtain a spreadsheet file, this parameter must be specified, and the display interval (see Section A.2) must be set to a non-zero value.
Output Options	Specifies the type of output(s) written to the spreadsheet file. One or more of the letters WINFS may be specified. See Appendix B.

Key word: DUMPR	
Input: History File	
History File	The name specifies a file (up to 17 characters) to which the program outputs for plotting are written. History file is an optional input. If omitted, the file will not be generated. Note that in order to obtain a history of the variables, this parameter must be specified, and the history interval (see Section A.2) must be set to a non-zero value.

Key word: RESTR	
Input: Restart File, Restart Time (see Section A.2)	
Restart File	The name specifies a file (up to 17 characters) from which the program reads data to restart the model. This data must have been generated (written) previously with the history parameter discussed earlier.
Restart Time (s)	A time step is given after the name of the file and specifies at what time the restart should occur.

A.4 Setting Ambient Conditions

The ambient conditions section of the input data allows the user to specify the temperature, pressure, and station elevation of the ambient atmosphere, as well as the absolute wind pressure to which the structure is subjected. There is an ambient for the interior and for the exterior of the structure. The key word for the interior of the structure is TAMB and for the exterior of the structure is EAMB. The form is the same for both.

The key word for the wind information is WIND. The wind modification is applied only to the vents which lead to the exterior. Pressure interior to a structure is calculated simply as a lapse rate based on the NOAA tables. This modification is applied to the vents which lead to the exterior ambient. The calculated pressure change is modified by the wind coefficient for each vent. This coefficient, which can vary from -1.0 to +1.0, nominally from -0.8 to +0.8, determines whether the vent is facing away from or into the wind. The pressure change is multiplied by the vent wind coefficient and added to the external ambient for each vent which is connected to the outside.

The choice for the station elevation, temperature and pressure must be consistent. Outside of that limitation, the choice is arbitrary. It is often convenient to choose the base of a structure to be at zero height and then reference the height of the structure with respect to that height. The temperature and pressure must then be measured at that position. Another possible choice would be the pressure and temperature at sea level, with the structure elevations then given with respect to mean sea level. This is also acceptable, but somewhat more tedious in specifying the construction of a structure. Either of these choices works though because consistent data for temperature and pressure are available from the Weather Service for either case.

If the EAMB or TAMB line is not included in the input file, default values are used. The WIND line is optional.

Example:

```
TAMB    300.   101300.       0.
EAMB    300.   101300.       0.
```

| Key words: EAMB and TAMB
| Inputs: Ambient Temperature, Ambient Pressure, Station Elevation
| (External and Internal, respectively) |

Ambient Temperature (K)	Ambient temperature is the temperature of the ambient atmosphere. Default is 300.
Ambient Pressure (Pa)	The ambient pressure is the pressure of the ambient atmosphere. Default is 101300.
Station Elevation (m)	The station elevation is the elevation of the point at which the ambient pressure and temperature (see above) are measured. The reference point for the elevation, pressure and temperature must be consistent. This is the reference datum for calculating the density of the atmosphere as well as the temperature and pressure inside and outside of the structure as a function of height. Default is 0.

| Key word: WIND
| Inputs: Wind Speed, Reference Height, Lapse Rate Coefficient |

Wind Speed (m/s)	Wind speed at the reference elevation. The default is 0.
Reference Height (m)	Height at which the reference wind speed is measured. The default is 10 m.
Lapse Rate Coefficient	The power law used to calculate the wind speed as a function of height. The default is 0.16.

A.5 Defining Compartments

This section allows the user to portray the geometry of the structure being modeled. The size and location of every compartment in the structure MUST be described. The maximum number of compartments is 15 compartments (plus the outdoors). The structure of the data is such that the compartments are described as entities, and then connected in appropriate ways. It is thus possible to have a set of compartments which can be configured in a variety of ways. In order to specify the geometry of a structure, it is necessary to give the physical characteristics. Thus the lines labelled HI/F, WIDTH, DEPTH and HEIGH are all required. Each of these lines requires "N" data entries, that is one for each compartment.

138

Example:

```
WIDTH    4.00    4.00
DEPTH    4.00    4.00
HEIGH    2.30    2.30
HI/F     0.00    2.30
```

Key word: WIDTH Input: Compartment Width	
Compartment Width (m)	Compartment width specifies the width of the compartment. The number of values on the line must equal the number of compartments in the simulation.

Key word: DEPTH Input: Compartment Depth	
Compartment Depth (m)	Compartment depth specifies the depth of the compartment. The number of values on the line must equal the number of compartments in the simulation.

Key word: HEIGH Input: Compartment Height	
Compartment Height (m)	Compartment Height specifies the height of the compartment. The number of values on the line must equal the number of compartments in the simulation.

Key word: HI/F Input: Floor Height	
Floor Height (m)	The floor height is the height of the floor of each compartment with respect to station elevation specified by the TAMB parameter. The reference point must be the same for all elevations in the input data. The number of values on the line must equal the number of compartments in the simulation.

A.6 Thermal Properties

The thermophysical properties of the enclosing surfaces are described by specifying the thermal conductivity, specific heat, emissivity, density, and thickness of the enclosing surfaces for each compartment. Currently, thermal properties for materials are read from a thermal database file unique to CFAST. The data in the file simply gives a name (such as CONCRETE) which is a pointer to the properties in the thermal database. The thermophysical properties are specified at *one* condition of temperature, humidity, etc. There can be as many as three layers per boundary, but they are specified in the thermal database itself.

If the thermophysical properties of the enclosing surfaces are not included, CFAST will treat them as adiabatic (no heat transfer). If a name is used which is not in the database, FAST will turn off the conduction calculation, and CFAST will stop with an appropriate error message.

Since most of the heat conduction is through the ceiling, and since the conduction calculation takes a significant fraction of the computation time, it is recommended that initial calculations be made using the ceiling only. Adding the walls generally has a small effect on the results, and the floor contribution is usually negligible. Clearly, there are cases where the above generalization does not hold, but it may prove to be a useful screening technique.

The default name for the thermal properties database is THERMAL.TPF. Another name can be used by selecting it during installation, or by using the key word THRMF in the CFAST data file.

Example:

```
CEILI GYPSUM    GYPSUM
WALLS PINEWOOD  PINEWOOD
FLOOR CONCRETE  CONCRETE
```

Key word: CEILI Inputs: Ceiling Materials	
Ceiling Materials	The label CEILI indicates that the names of thermophysical properties on this line describe the ceiling material. If this parameter is present, there must be an entry for each compartment.

Key word: WALLS Inputs: Wall Materials	
Wall Materials	The label WALLS indicates that the names of thermophysical properties on this line describe the wall material. If this parameter is present, there must be an entry for each compartment.

Key word: FLOOR Inputs: Floor Materials	
Floor Materials	The label FLOOR indicates that the names of thermophysical properties on this line describe the floor material. If this parameter is present, there must be an entry for each compartment.

Key word: THRMF Input: Thermal Database	
Thermal Database	The name specifies a file (up to 12 characters) from which the program reads thermophysical data. If this parameter is not specified, then either the default (THERMAL.DAT) is used, or the name is read from the configuration file.

A.7 Defining Connections for Horizontal Flow

This section of the input data file is required to specify horizontal flow connections between compartments in the structure. These may include doors between compartments or windows in the compartments (between compartments or to the outdoors). These specifications do **not** correspond to physically connecting the walls between specified compartments. Lack of an opening prevents flow between the compartments. Openings to the outside are included as openings to a compartment with a number one greater than the number of compartments described in the Geometry section. The key word is HVENT. If the HVENT line is entered, the first six entries on the line are required. There is an optional seventh parameter to specify a wind coefficient. The soffit and sill specifications are with respect to the first compartment specified and is not symmetric. Reversing the order of the compartment designations does make a difference.

Horizontal flow vents may be opened or closed during the fire with the use of the CVENT key word. The initial format of CVENT is similar to HVENT specifying the connecting compartments and vent number. Each CVENT line in the input file details the open/close time dependent characteristics for one horizontal flow vent by specifying a fractional value for each LFMAX time entry. The default is 1.0 which is a fully open vent. A value of 0.5 would specify a vent which was halfway open.

Example:

```
HVENT   1   3   1     1.07     2.00     0.00     0.00
HVENT   2   3   1     1.07     2.00     1.00     0.00
CVENT   1   3   1     1.00     1.00
CVENT   2   3   1     1.00     1.00
```

Key word: HVENT	
Inputs: First Compartment, Second Compartment, Vent Number, Width, Soffit, Sill, Wind	
First Compartment	The first compartment is simply the first connection.
Second Compartment	The second compartment is the compartment number to which the first compartment is connected. The order has one significance. The height of the sill and soffit are with respect to the first compartment specified.
Vent Number	There can be as many as four vents between any two compartments. This number specifies which vent is being described. It can range from one to four.
Width (m)	The width of the opening.
Soffit (m)	Position of the top of the opening above the floor of the compartment number specified as the first compartment.
Sill (m)	Sill height is the height of the bottom of the opening above the floor of the compartment number specified as the first compartment.
Wind	Optional parameter, the wind coefficient is the cosine of the angle between the wind vector and the vent opening. This applies only to vents which connect to the outside ambient (specified with EAMB). The range of values is -1.0 to +1.0. If omitted, the value defaults to zero.
First Compartment Position	Optional parameter, horizontal distance between the centerline of this vent and the reference point in the first compartment
Second Compartment Position	Optional parameter, horizontal distance between the centerline of this vent and the reference point in the second compartment

Key word: CVENT	
Inputs: First Compartment, Second Compartment, Vent Number, Width	
First Compartment	The first compartment.
Second Compartment	The second compartment is the compartment number to which the first compartment is connected.
Vent Number	This number specifies which vent is being described. It can range from one to four.
Width	Fraction that the vent is open. This applies to the width only. The sill and soffit are not changed. The number of values on the line must equal the number of points on the fire timeline.

A.8 Defining Connections for Vertical Flow

The Vents(ceiling,...) section of the input data file describes any vertical flow openings, such as scuddles, between compartments in the structure (or between a compartment and the outdoors). Openings to the outside are included as openings to a compartment with a number one greater than the number of compartments described in the Geometry section. Each VVENT line in the input file describes one vertical vent. There are four parameters, the connected compartments, the shape of the opening, and the effective area of the vent. At the present time, there is not an equivalent CVENT mechanism for opening or closing the vertical vents.

Example:

```
VVENT    2   1  1.00    1
```

Key word: VVENT	
Inputs: First Compartment, Second Compartment, Area, Shape	
First Compartment	The first compartment is simply the first connection.
Second Compartment	The second compartment is the compartment number to which the first compartment is connected.
Area (m^2)	This is the effective area of the opening. For a hole, it would be the actual opening. For a diffuser, the effective area is somewhat less than the geometrical size of the opening.
Shape	1 for circle or 2 for square.

A.9 Adding Sprinklers and Detectors

Sprinklers and detectors are both considered detection devices by the FAST model and are handled using the same input keywords. Detection is based upon heat transfer to the detector. Fire suppression by a user-specified water spray begins once the associated detection device is activated. A maximum of 20 sprinklers or detectors can be included for any input file and model run. These can be in one compartment or scattered throughout the structure. The DETECT keyword is used for both detectors and sprinklers.

Key word: DETECT Inputs: Detector Type, Compartment, Activation Temperature, Depth Position, Breadth Position, Height Position, RTI, Sprinkler, Spray Density	
Detector Type	Type of detector.
Compartment	The compartment in which the detector or sprinkler is located.
Activation Temperature (K)	The temperature at or above which the detector link activates.
Depth Position (m)	Position of the detector or sprinkler as a distance from the rear wall of the compartment (X direction). Default value is ½ compartment depth.
Breadth Position (m)	Position of the object as a distance from the left wall of the compartment (Y direction). Default value is ½ compartment breadth.
Height Position (m)	Position of the object as a distance from the floor of the compartment (Z direction). Default value is compartment depth.
RTI $((m \cdot s)^{1/2})$	The Response Time Index (RTI) for the sprinkler or detection device.
Sprinkler	If set to a value of 1, the sprinkler will quench the fire with the specified spray density of water.
Spray Density (m/s)	The amount of water dispersed by a water spray-sprinkler. The units for spray density are length/time. These units are derived by dividing the volumetric rate of water flow by the area protected by the water spray. The spray density may be measured by collecting water in a pan located within the spray area and recording the rate-of-rise in the water level.

A.10 Defining the Fire and Time-Dependent Fire Curves

The fire specifications allow the user to describe the fire source in the simulation. The location and position of the fire are specified using the LFBO and FPOS lines. Chemical properties of the fuel are specified with the CHEMI key word along with miscellaneous parameters. Turn the ceiling jet calculations on by using the CJET key word. By default, the ceiling jet is not included in a CFAST simulation.

By default, the fire is placed in the center of the compartment on the floor. To place the fire in a different location, the FPOS key word may be included in the input file. If values for any of the three variables are invalid (i.e., less than zero or greater than the compartment dimension in the appropriate direction), the location for that direction defaults to the center of the appropriate direction.

CFAST no longer supports use of the LFMAX key word in the data file. LFMAX is now determined by the number of entries on the FTIME line used to specify points of the fire timeline. The time dependent variables of the fire are described with a series of mass loss rate, rate of heat release, fuel height, and fuel area inputs. All of these specifications are optional. If entered, a total of LFMAX+1 values must be included for each time dependent input line. The defaults shown for each key word reflect the values for methane.

With the three parameters, the heat of combustion (HOC) from CHEMI, FMASS and FQDOT, the pyrolysis and heat release rate are over specified. The model uses the last two of the three to obtain the third parameter. That is, if the three were specified in the order HOC, FMASS and FQDOT, then FQDOT would be divided by FMASS to obtain the HOC for each time interval. If the order were FMASS, FQDOT and HOC, then the pyrolysis rate would be determined by dividing the heat release rate by the heat of combustion. If only two of the three are given, then those two will determine the third, and finally, if none or only one of the parameters is present, the defaults shown are used.

Species production rates are specified in a manner similar to the fire, entering the rates as a series of points with respect to time. The species which are followed by CFAST are:

- Carbon Dioxide
- Carbon Monoxide
- Concentration-Time Product
- Hydrogen Cyanide
- Hydrogen Chloride
- Nitrogen
- Oxygen
- Soot (Smoke Density)
- Total Unburned Hydrocarbons
- Water

The program performs a linear interpolation between the time points to determine the time of interest.

For a type one (LFBT=1) fire, only the concentration-time product of pyrolysate (CT) can be specified. No other species are followed. For a type two (LFBT=2) fire, nitrogen (N2), oxygen (O2), carbon dioxide (CO2), carbon monoxide (CO), hydrogen cyanide (HCN), hydrogen chloride (HCL), soot (OD), unburned fuel and water (H2O) are followed. For a type two fire, HCN, HCL, CT, O2, OD, CO and the hydrogen to carbon ratio (HCR) can be specified. In all cases, the unit of the production rates is kg/kg. However, the meaning of the production rates is different for the several types of species. See the discussion for each species key word below for the meaning of the corresponding production rate.

Example:

```
CHEMI   16.     0.   10.0     18100000.  300. 400.   0.
LFBO    1
LFBT    2
FPOS    2.00    2.00    0.00
FTIME   400.
FMASS   0.0014 0.0014
FHIGH   0.00    0.01
FAREA   0.00    0.00
FQDOT   2.53E+04 2.53E+04
CJET    OFF
HCR     0.333 0.333
CO      0.010 0.010
```

Key word: CHEMI	
Inputs: Molar Weight, Relative Humidity, Lower Oxygen Limit, Heat of Combustion, Initial Fuel Temperature, Gaseous Ignition Temperature, Radiative Fraction	
Molar Weight	Molecular weight of the fuel vapor. This is the conversion factor from mass density to molecular density for "tuhc." Default is 16. It is used only for conversion to ppm, and has no effect on the model itself.
Relative Humidity (percent)	The initial relative humidity in the system. This is converted to kilograms of water per cubic meter.
Lower Oxygen Limit (percent)	The limit on the ratio of oxygen to other gases in the system below which a flame will not burn. This is applicable only to type (LFBT) 2 or later fires. The default is 10.
Heat of Combustion (J/kg)	Heat of combustion of the fuel. Default is 50000000.
Initial Fuel Temperature (K)	Typically, the initial fuel temperature is the same as the ambient temperature as specified in the ambient conditions section.
Gaseous Ignition Temperature (K)	Minimum temperature for ignition of the fuel as it flows from a compartment through a vent into another compartment. If omitted, the default is arbitrarily set to the initial fuel temperature plus 100K.
Radiative Fraction	The fraction of heat released by the fire that goes into radiation. Default is 0.30.

Key word: FAREA	
Inputs: Fuel Area	
Fuel Area (m)	The area of the fire at the base of the flames.

Key word: FHIGH Inputs: Fuel Height	
Fuel Height (m)	The height of the base of the flames above the floor of the compartment of fire origin for each point of the specified fire.

Key word: FMASS Inputs: Mass Loss Rate	
Mass Loss Rate (kg/s)	The rate at which fuel is pyrolyzed at times corresponding to each point of the specified fire.

Key word: FPOS Inputs: Depth, Breadth, Height (relative to the left rear corner of the compartment – see figure above)	
Depth	Position of the fire as a distance from the rear wall of the compartment (X direction).
Breadth	Position of the fire as a distance from the left wall of the compartment (Y direction).
Height	Height of the fire above the floor (Z direction). This value is simply added to the fire height at each time specified by the FHIGH key word.

Key word: FQDOT Inputs: Heat Release Rate	
Heat Release Rate (W)	The heat release rate of the specified fire.

Key word: FTIME Inputs: Time Points	
Time Points (s)	An entry indicates a point on the timeline where mass loss rate, fuel height and species are specified for the fire. This time is indepen-

Key word: LFBO	
Input: Compartment of Fire Origin	
Compartment of Fire Origin	Compartment of fire origin is the compartment number in which the fire originates. Default is 0. The outside can not be specified as a compartment. An entry of 0 turns off the main fire leaving only object fires specified by the OBJECT key word.

Key word: LFBT	
Input: Fire Type	
Fire Type	This is a number indicating the type of fire. 1 Unconstrained fire 2 Constrained fire. The default is 1. See section 3.10 for a discussion of the implications of this choice.

Key words: HCN, HCL, CT, HCR, or O2	
Inputs: Composition of the Pyrolyzed Fuel	
Production Rate (kg/kg)	Units are kilogram of species produced per kilogram of fuel pyrolyzed for HCN and HCL. The input for CT is the kilograms of "toxic" combustion products produced per kilogram of fuel pyrolyzed. Input for HCR is the mass ratio of hydrogen to carbon ratio in the fuel. Input for O2 is the mass ratio of oxygen to carbon *as it becomes available from the fuel*. The O2 input thus represents excess oxygen available from the fuel for combustion. For normal fuels, this input should be left out.

Key words: OD and CO Inputs: Yield	
Yield (kg/kg)	Input the ratio of the mass of carbon to carbon dioxide produced by the oxidation of the fuel for OD. The input for CO is the ratio of the mass of carbon monoxide to carbon dioxide produced by the oxidation of the fuel.

A.11 Building HVAC Systems

These key words are used to describe a mechanical ventilation system. The MVOPN line is used to connect a compartment to a node in the mechanical ventilation system. The elevation for each of these exterior nodes is specified as a relative height to the compartment floor on the MVOPN line. The MVDCT key word is used to specify a piece of the mechanical ventilation duct work. CAUTION: Nodes specified by each MVDCT entry must connect with other nodes, fans, or compartments. Do not specify ducts which are isolated from the rest of the system. Specify interior elevations of the mechanical ventilation nodes using the INELV line. All node elevations can be specified, but elevations for the exterior nodes, that is those connected to a compartment, are ignored. These heights are determined by entries on the MVOPN line. The heights for interior nodes are absolute heights above the reference datum specified by TAMB. The heights are specified in pairs with the node number followed by the height.

A fan is defined using the MVFAN line to indicate node numbers and to specify the fan curve with power law coefficients. There must be at least one and a maximum of five coefficients specified for each MVFAN entry. The fan coefficients are simply the coefficients of an interpolating polynomial for the flow speed as a function of the pressure across the fan housing. In this example, the coefficients:

```
B( 1) =    0.140E+00       b(1)
B( 2) =   -0.433E-03       b(2) x p
```

were calculated from entries made in FAST:

```
                PRESSURE          FLOW

Minimum            0.00         0.1400
Maximum          300.00         0.0101
```

Example:

```
MVOPN   1   1 V   2.10    0.12
MVOPN   2   3 V   2.10    0.12
MVDCT   1   2   2.30    0.10 .00200    0.00 1.0000    0.00 1.0000
```

```
MVFAN   2   3   0.00 300.00  0.140E+00 -0.433E-03
INELV   1   2.10   2   4.40   3   4.40
```

Key word: INELV Inputs: Node Number, Height	
Node Number	Number of an interior node.
Height (m)	Height of the node with respect to the height of the reference datum, specified by TAMB or EAMB.

Key word: MVDCT **Inputs:** First Node Number, Second Node Number, Length, Diameter, Absolute Roughness, First Flow Coefficient, First Area, Second Flow Coefficient, Second Area	
First Node Number	First node number. This is a node in the mechanical ventilation scheme, not a compartment number (see MVOPN).
Second Node Number	Second node number.
Length (m)	Length of the duct.
Diameter (m)	All duct work is assumed to be circular. Other shapes must be approximated by changing the flow coefficient. This is done implicitly by network models of mechanical ventilation and forced flow, but must be done explicitly here.
Absolute Roughness (m)	Roughness of the duct.
First Flow Coefficient	Flow coefficient to allow for an expansion or contraction at the end of the duct which is connected to node number one. To use a straight through connection (no expansion or contraction) set to zero.
First Area (m²)	Area of the expanded joint.
Second Flow Coefficient	Coefficient for second node.
Second Area (m²)	Area at the second node.

Key word:	MVFAN
Inputs: First Node, Second Node, Minimum Pressure, Maximum Pressure, Coefficients	
First Node	First node in the mechanical ventilation system to which the fan is connected.
Second Node	Second node to which the fan is connected.
Minimum Pressure (Pa)	Lowest pressure of the fan curve. Below this value, the flow is assumed to be constant.
Maximum Pressure (Pa)	Highest pressure at which the fan will operate. Above this point, the flow is assumed to stop.
Coefficients	At least one, and a maximum of five coefficients, to specify the flow as a function of pressure.

Key word:	MVOPN
Inputs: Compartment Number, Duct Work Node Number, Orientation, Height, Area	
Compartment Number	Specify the compartment number.
Duct Work Node Number	Corresponding node in the mechanical ventilation system to which the compartment is to be connected.
Orientation	V for vertical or H for horizontal.
Height (m)	Height of the duct opening above the floor of the compartment.
Area (m^2)	Area of the opening into the compartment.

A.12 Selection of Ceiling Jet Surfaces

Key word: CJET Input: OFF, CEILING, WALL, or ALL	
Current Setting	To include the calculation for the ceiling, wall, or both surfaces, the CJET key word is used together with one of the identifiers CEILING, WALL, or ALL. For example, to turn the ceiling on, use "CJET CEILING". At present, this key word effects only the calculation of the convective heating boundary condition for the conduction routines. If a particular surface is ON, the ceiling jet algorithm is used to determine the convective heating of the surface. If OFF, the bulk temperature of the upper layer determines the convective heating.

A.13 Additional Burning Objects

The OBJECT key word allows the specification of additional objects to be burned in the fire scenario. The object name and object compartment are required if the OBJECT key word is used. All other input items have default values if they are not specified. These defaults are: start time 0.0, first element 1, depth (x position) one half the depth of the compartment, breadth (y position) one half the width of the compartment, and height (z position) 0.0. To specify any input item, all preceding items on the OBJECT line must also be specified. For example, the first element can not be set if start time is not set. Positioning of the object within a compartment is specified in the same manner as for the main fire. See figure below.

EXAMPLE:

```
OBJECT  SOFA        1      10   1    4.00    2.00    0.00
OBJECT  WARDROBE    1      30   3    0.00    2.00    0.00
```

Key word: OBJFL Input: Objects Database	
Objects Database	The name specifies a file (up to 17 characters) from which the program obtains object data. If this parameter is not specified, then either the default (OBJECTS.DAT) is used, or the name is read from the configuration file.

Key word: OBJECT
Inputs: Object Name, Object Compartment, Ignition Criterion Value, Ignition Criterion Type, Depth Position, Breadth Position, Height Position, Normal Vector (Depth), Normal Vector (Breadth), Normal Vector (Height), Horizontal Flame Spread Ignition Position, Vertical Flame Spread Ignition Position

Object Name	The name from the objects database for the desired object. Specifying a name not found in the database causes CFAST to stop with an appropriate error message. FAST considers such an object undefined and does not display the entry.
Object Compartment	The compartment that the object is in during the simulation. If a compartment number outside the range of specified compartments is used, CFAST provides an error message and stops. FAST considers such an object undefined and does not display the entry.
Ignition Criterion Value	The numerical value at which ignition will occur. If it is less than or equal to zero, the default is taken. For constrained and unconstrained fires, the default is and ignition at time of zero. For flame spread objects, the default is the ignition temperature in the database.
Ignition Criterion Type	The type of ignition condition specified by the *Ignition Criterion Value*. Acceptable values are 1 for time, 2 for object surface temperature, and 3 for incident flux to object surface.
Depth Position	Position of the object as a distance from the rear wall of the object compartment (X direction). Default value is ½ compartment depth.
Breadth Position	Position of the object as a distance from the left wall of the object compartment (Y direction). Default value is ½ compartment breadth.
Height Position	Height of the object above the floor (Z direction). Default value is 0.
Normal Vector (Depth)	Specifies a vector of unit length perpendicular to the exposed surface of the object. (Depth) component is in the direction from the rear wall of the object compartment. Default value is a horizontal, upward facing object, unit vector = (0,0,1)
Normal Vector (Breadth)	Specifies a vector of unit length perpendicular to the exposed surface of the object. (Breadth) component is in the direction from the left wall of the object compartment. Default value is a horizontal, upward facing object, unit vector = (0,0,1)

Normal Vector (Height)	Specifies a vector of unit length perpendicular to the exposed surface of the object. (Breadth) component is in the direction from the floor of the object compartment. Default value is a horizontal, upward facing object, unit vector = (0,0,1)
Horizontal Flame Spread Ignition Position	Assuming the ignition surface is a wall with the corner closest to the lower back left corner of the compartment, the horizontal flame spread ignition position is the horizontal distance from the rear lower corner of the object. Only applicable to flame spread objects.
Vertical Flame Spread Ignition Position	Assuming the ignition surface is a wall with the corner closest to the lower back left corner of the compartment, the horizontal flame spread ignition position is the vertical distance from the rear lower corner of the object. Only applicable to flame spread objects.

A.14 Ceiling to Floor Heat Transfer

Ceiling to floor conduction informs the fire model that heat transfer between the ceiling and floor of specified compartments is to be accounted for in the simulation. Ceiling to floor heat transfer occurs between interior compartments of the structure or between an interior compartment and the outdoors.

Key word: CFCON	
Input: First Compartment, Second Compartment	
First Compartment	First of the connected compartments. Order of the inputs is not important
Second Compartment	Second of the connected compartments. Order of the inputs is not important

A.15 Defining Targets

CFAST can track and report calculations of the heat flux striking and the temperature of arbitrarily positioned and oriented targets. Two keywords are used to specify targets: The TARGET keyword is used to specify arbitrary targets placed anywhere in a compartment. The TARG keyword is used to specify targets on the interior bounding surface of a compartment.

Key word: TARGET Input: Compartment, Depth Position, Breadth Position, Height Position, Normal Vector (Depth), Normal Vector (Breadth), Normal Vector (Height), Material, Method, Equation Type	
Compartment	The compartment in which the target is located
Depth Position	Position of the target as a distance from the rear wall of the target compartment (X direction). Default value is ½ compartment depth.
Breadth Position	Position of the target as a distance from the left wall of the target compartment (Y direction). Default value is ½ compartment breadth.
Height Position	Height of the target above the floor (Z direction). Default value is 0.
Normal Vector (Depth)	Specifies a vector of unit length perpendicular to the exposed surface of the target. (Depth) component in the direction from the rear wall of the target compartment. Default value is a horizontal, upward facing target, unit vector = (0,0,1)
Normal Vector (Breadth)	Specifies a vector of unit length perpendicular to the exposed surface of the target. (Breadth) component in the direction from the left wall of the target compartment. Default value is a horizontal, upward facing target, unit vector = (0,0,1)
Normal Vector (Height)	Specifies a vector of unit length perpendicular to the exposed surface of the target. (Breadth) component in the direction from the floor of the target compartment. Default value is a horizontal, upward facing target, unit vector = (0,0,1)
Material	An optional parameter used to specify the wall material of the target. Any material from the thermal database used to represent wall materials may be used here. Since the transient heat conduction problem is not solved now for the target this parameter is not used.

Method	indicates the solution method
	    STEADY for steady state
	    XPLICIT for explicit (as is done with species)
	    MPLICIT for implicit (as is done with all other variables)
	
	Default method is MPLICIT

Equation Type	If METHOD is not STEADY, this parameter further indicates the equation type to be either ODE or PDE. The default is PDE

Key word:	TARG
Input: Compartment, Surface, Depth Position, Breadth Position, Method, Equation Type	
Compartment	The compartment in which the target is located
Surface	Surface defines the compartment surface for the target. It is one of the character strings, UP, FRONT, RIGHT, BACK, LEFT and DOWN
Depth Position	Position of the target as a distance from the rear wall of the target compartment (X direction). Default value is ½ compartment depth.
Breadth Position	Position of the target as a distance from the left wall of the target compartment (Y direction). Default value is ½ compartment breadth.

Method	indicates the solution method
	        STEADY for steady state
	        XPLICIT for explicit (as is done with species)
	        MPLICIT for implicit (as is done with all other variables)
	
	Default method is MPLICIT

Equation Type	If METHOD is not STEADY, this parameter further indicates the equation type to be either ODE or PDE. The default is PDE

A.16 Modeling Compartment as a Shaft or Hallway

For stairwells, elevator shafts, and similar compartments, the use of a single, well-mixed zone better approximates conditions within the compartment. To specify use of a one zone model for individual compartments rather than the typical two zone model, the SHAFT keyword is used.

Example:

SHAFT 1

Key word:	SHAFT
Input: Compartment	
Compartment	Compartment to be modeled as a single, well-mixed zone

For long hallways or corridors, there can be a significant delay time for the initial hot gas layer to travel along the ceiling to the far end of the compartment. To allow the CFAST model to calculate the ceiling jet velocity and temperature along the corridor and its effects on heat transfer to the ceiling, the HALL keyword is used. In addition, the horizontal position of the vents in the compartment are also specified with the HVENT keyword.

Example:

HALL 1

Key word: HALL	
Input: Compartment, Velocity, Depth, Decay Distance	
Compartment	Compartment to be modeled as a single, well-mixed zone
Velocity	Optional parameter, ceiling jet velocity at the distance from the reference point where the temperature falls off by 50 percent.
Depth	Optional parameter, ceiling jet depth at the distance from the reference point where the temperature falls off by 50 percent.
Decay Distance	Optional parameter, distance from the reference point where the temperature falls off by 50 percent.

A.17 Runtime Graphics

A graphics specification can be added to the data file. Details of the meaning of some of the parameters is best left to the discussion of the device independent graphics software used by CFAST. However, the information necessary to use it is straightforward. The general structure is similar to that used for the compartment and fire specification. One must tell the program "what to plot," "how it should appear," and "where to put it."

The key words for "where to put it" are:

DEVICE	where to plot it
BAR	bar charts
GRAPH	specify an x-y plot
TABLE	put the data into a table
PALETTE	specify the legend for CAD views
VIEW	show a perspective picture of the structure
WINDOW	the size of the window in "user" space.

The complete key word is required. That is, for the "where to put it" terms, no abbreviations are allowed. Then one must specify the variables to be plotted. They are:

VENT, HEAT, PRESSUR, WALL, TEMPERA, INTERFA,
H_2O, CO_2, CO, OD, O_2, TUHC, HCN, HCL, CT

As might be expected, these are similar key words to those used in the plotting program, CPlot. In this case, it is a reduced set. The application and use of CFAST and CPlot are different.

For each key word there are parameters to specify the location of the graph, the colors and finally, titles as appropriate. For the variables, there is a corresponding pointer to the graph of interest.

The WINDOW label specifies the user space for placement of graphs, views, etc. The most common values (which are also the default) are:

Xl = 0., Yb = 0., Zf = 0.
Xr = 1279., Yt = 1023., Zb = 10.

This is not a required parameter; however, it is often convenient to define graphs in terms of the units that are used. For example, if one wished to display a house in terms of a blueprint, the more natural units might be feet. In that case, the parameters might have the values:

Xl = 0., Yb = 0., Zf = 0.
Xr = 50., Yt = 25., Zb = 30.

Up to five graphs, tables, bar charts, and views may be displayed at one time on the graphics display. Up to five labels may be displayed at one time on the graphics display. Each type of output and each label is identified by a unique number (1-5) and placed in the window at a specified location. Xl, Yb, Zf, Xr, Yt and Zb have a meaning similar to WINDOW. However, here they specify where in the window to put the output.

The PALETTE label performs a specialized function for showing colors on the views. A four entry table is created and used for each type of filling polygon used in a view. Up to five palettes may be defined. Each palette is identified by a unique number and placed in the window at a specified location. Xl, Yb, Zf, Xr, Yt and Zb have a meaning similar to WINDOW. However, here they specify where in the window to put the palette.

In order to see the variables, they must be assigned to one of the above displays. This is accomplished with the variable pointers as:

```
(Variable) (nmopq) (Compartment) (Layer).
```

Variable is one of the available variables VENT, HEAT, PRESSUR, WALL, TEMPERA, INTERFA, N_2, O_2, CO_2, CO, HCN, HCL, TUHC, H_2O, OD, CT used as a label for the line. The species listed correspond to the variable "SPECIES" in CPlot. (nmopqr) is a vector which points to:

```
index    display in

(1) n -> bar chart
(2) m -> table
(3) o -> view
(4) p -> label
(5) q -> graph
```

respectively. These numbers vary from 1 to 5 and correspond to the value of "n" in the "where to put it" specification. Compartment is the compartment number of the variable and Layer is "U" or "L" for upper and lower layer, respectively.

Example:

```
WINDOW          0      0  -100  1280  1024  1100
GRAPH 1  100.  050.  0.  600.  475.  10.  3 TIME   HEIGHT
GRAPH 2  100.  550.  0.  600.  940.  10.  3 TIME   CELSIUS
GRAPH 3  720.  050.  0.  1250.  475.  10.  3 TIME   FIRE_SIZE(kW)
GRAPH 4  720.  550.  0.  1250.  940.  10.  3 TIME   O|D2|O(%)
INTERFA 0 0 0 0 1    1 U
TEMPERA 0 0 0 0 2    1 U
HEAT    0 0 0 0 3    1 U
O2      0 0 0 0 4    1 U
INTERFA 0 0 0 0 1    2 U
TEMPERA 0 0 0 0 2    2 U
HEAT    0 0 0 0 3    2 U
O2      0 0 0 0 4    2 U
```

Key word: DEVICE Input: Plotting Device	
Plotting Device	The Plotting Device specifies the hardware device where the graphics is to be displayed. It is installation dependent. In general it specifies which device will receive the output. For most systems, 1 is for the screen from which keyboard input comes, and 6 is for the hpgl files.

161

Key word: WINDOW	
Inputs: Xl, Yb, Zf, Xr, Yt, Zb	
Xl	Left hand side of the window in any user desired units.
Yb	Bottom of the window in any user desired units.
Zf	Forward edge of the 3D block in any user desired units.
Xr	Right hand side of the window in any user desired units.
Yt	Top of the window in any user desired units.
Zb	Rear edge of the 3D block in any user desired units. These definitions refer to the 3D plotting block that can be seen.

Key word: BAR	
Inputs: Bar Chart Number, Xl, Yb, Zf, Xr, Yt, Zb, Abscissa Title, Ordinate Title	
Bar Chart Number	The number to identify the bar chart. Allowable values are from 1 to 5.
Xl	Left hand side of the bar chart within the window in the same units as that of the window.
Yb	Bottom of the bar chart within the window in the same units as that of the window.
Zf	Forward edge of the 3D block within the window in the same units as that of the window.
Xr	Right hand side of the bar chart within the window in the same units as that of the window.
Yt	Top of the bar chart within the window in the same units as that of the window.
Zb	Back edge of the 3D block within the window in the same units as that of the window.
Abscissa Title	Title for the abscissa (horizontal axis). To have blanks in the title, use the underscore character "_".
Ordinate Title	Title for the ordinate (vertical axis). To have blanks in the title, use the underscore character "_".

Key word: GRAPH **Inputs:** Graph Number, Xl, Yb, Zf, Xr, Yt, Zb, Color, Abscissa Title, Ordinate Title	
Graph Number	The number to identify the graph. Allowable values are from 1 to 5. The graphs must be numbered consecutively, although they do not have to be given in order. It is acceptable to define graph 4 before graph 2, but if graph 4 is to be used, then graphs 1 through 3 must also be defined.
Xl	Left hand side of the graph within the window in the same units as that of the window.
Yb	Bottom of the graph within the window in the same units as that of the window.
Zf	Forward edge of the 3D (three dimensional) block within the window in the same units as that of the window.
Xr	Right hand side of the graph within the window in the same units as that of the window.
Yt	Top of the graph within the window in the same units as that of the window.
Zf	Back edge of the 3D block within the window in the same units as that of the window.
Color	The color of the graph and labels which is specified as an integer from 1 to 15. Refer to DEVICE (NBSIR 85-3235) for the colors corresponding to the color values.
Abscissa Title	Title for the abscissa (horizontal axis). To have blanks in the title, use the underscore character "_".
Ordinate Title	Title for the ordinate (vertical axis). To have blanks in the title, use the underscore character "_".

Key word: TABLE Inputs: Table Number, Xl, Yb, Zf, Xr, Yt, Zb	
Table Number	The table number is the number to identify the table. Allowable values are from 1 to 5. The tables must be numbered consecutively, although they do not have to be given in order. It is acceptable to define table 4 before table 2, but if table 4 is to be used, then tables 1 through 3 must also be defined.
Xl	Left hand side of the table within the window in the same units as that of the window.
Yb	Bottom of the table within the window in the same units as that of the window.
Zf	Forward edge of the 3D block within the window in the same units as that of the window.
Xr	Right hand side of the table within the window in the same units as that of the window.
Yt	Top of the table within the window in the same units as that of the window.
Zb	Back edge of the 3D block within the window in the same units as that of the window.

Key word: VIEW Inputs: View Number, Xl, Yb, Zf, Xr, Yt, Zb, File, Transform Matrix	
View Number	View number is the number to identify the view. Allowable values are from 1 to 5. The views must be numbered consecutively, although they do not have to be given in order. It is acceptable to define view 4 before view 2, but if view 4 is to be used, then views 1 through 3 must also be defined.
Xl	Left hand side of the view within the window in the same units as that of the window.
Yb	Bottom of the view within the window in the same units as that of the window.
Zf	Forward edge of the 3D block within the window in the same units as that of the window.
Xr	Right hand side of the view within the window in the same units as that of the window.
Yt	Top of the view within the window in the same units as that of the window.
Zf	Back edge of the 3D block within the window in the same units as that of the window.
File	File is the filename of a building descriptor file.
Transform Matrix	The Transform Matrix is a 16 number matrix which allows dynamic positioning of the view within the window. The matrix (1 0 0 0 0 1 0 0 0 0 1 0 0 0 0 1) would show the image as it would appear in a display from BUILD.

Key word:	LABEL
Inputs: Label Number, Xl, Yb, Zf, Xr, Yt, Zb, Text, Angle1, Angle2	
Label Number	Label number is the number to identify the label. Allowable values are from 1 to 5.
Xl	Left hand side of the label within the window in the same units as that of the window.
Yb	Bottom of the label within the window in the same units as that of the window.
Zf	Forward edge of the 3D block within the window in the same units as that of the window.
Xr	Right hand side of the label within the window in the same units as that of the window.
Yt	Top of the label within the window in the same units as that of the window.
Zb	Back edge of the 3D block within the window in the same units as that of the window.
Text	The text to be displayed within the label. To have blanks in the title, use the underscore character "_".
Color	Color of the text to be displayed (a number from 0 to 15).
Angle1 and Angle2	Angles for display of the label in a right cylindrical coordinate space. At present, only the first angle is used and represents a positive counterclockwise rotation; set the second angle to zero. Both angles are in radians.

Key word: PALETTE Inputs: Palette Number, Xl, Yb, Zf, Xr, Yt, Zb, Color and Label	
Palette Number	Palette number is the number to identify the palette. Allowable values are from 1 to 5.
Xl	Left hand side of the palette within the window in the same units as that of the window.
Yb	Bottom of the palette within the window in the same units as that of the window.
Zf	Forward edge of the 3D block within the window in the same units as that of the window.
Xr	Right hand side of the palette within the window in the same units as that of the window.
Yt	Top of the palette within the window in the same units as that of the window.
Zb	Back edge of the 3D block within the window in the same units as that of the window.
Color and Label	There are four pairs of color/text combinations, each corresponding to an entry in the palette. The color number is an integer from 1 to 15 and the text can be up to 50 characters (total line length of 128 characters maximum). As before, spaces are indicated with an underscore character "_".

Appendix B FAST Program and Command Line Parameters

B.1 Numerical Parameters

FAST is intended for use with a wide variety of fire scenarios. A number of numerical limits in the software implementation of the model are noted below

Maximum simulation time in seconds	86 400
Maximum number of compartments	30
Maximum number of object fires which can be included in a single test case	30
Maximum number of object fire definitions which can be included in a single object fire database file	30
Maximum number of material thermal property definitions which can be included in a single thermal database file	56
Maximum number of slabs in a single surface material in the thermal database file	3
Maximum total number of fans in all mechanical ventilation systems which can be included in a single test case	5
Maximum total number of ducts in all mechanical ventilation systems which can be included in a single test case	62
Maximum total number of connections between compartments and mechanical ventilation systems which can be included in a single test case	62
Maximum number of independent mechanical ventilation systems which can be included in a single test case	10
Maximum number of targets which can be included in a single test case. In addition, the CFAST model includes a target on the floor of each compartment in the simulation and one for each object fire in simulation.	30
Maximum number of data points in a history or spreadsheet file	900

B.2 Command Line Parameters

The CFAST model and other individual routines can be run directly from the DOS command line. The format of the command line for CFAST is as follows:

```
CFAST <input file> <output file> <options>
```

where

<input file>: is the name of the input data file contains a series of lines which define the simulation. See Appendix A for details of the CFAST input keywords.

<output file>: is the name of the file to which any specified text output will be written.

<options>: specify any output reporting or other options to control the output of the program. The options available are as follows:

/k – directs that CFAST should ignore any input from the keyboard. This option is useful mainly for running a number of test cases in batch mode

/l – directs that CFAST should generate an error log file named CFAST.LOG which contains detailed debugging information.

/n – directs that CFAST should not print out the normal header to the console at the beginning of a simulation. This option is useful mainly for running a number of test cases in batch mode

/r – directs cfast to includes additional variables in any text or spreadsheet output. The /r is followed by one or more of the following characters to indicate the level of output:

> w – include wall surface and target fluxes in the output
> i – include model initial conditions and scenario description in the output
> n – include "normal" printout of layer temperatures, interface height, and fire size in the output
> f – include vent flows in the output
> s – include layer and wall surface species concentrations in the output
> t – include tenability estimates for each compartment in the output
> p – include wall temperature profiles in the output

Thus, the option /rwinfstp would include the most complete test or spreadsheet output.

These output options also apply to the programs report and reportss.

B.3 Output Units

In the GUI interface, the user can specify the units displayed for most input parameters. Outputs from CFAST, report, and reportss are in S.I. units. The following shows the units for output variables for a simple example.

Time =   1200.0 seconds.

Compartment	Upper Temp. (K)	Lower Temp. (K)	Inter. Height (m)	Upper Vol. (m^3)	Upper Absorb (m^-1)	Lower Absorb (m^-1)	Pressure (Pa)	Ambient Target (W/m^2)	Floor Target (W/m^2)
1	875.5	439.1	0.7806	15. (68%)	0.000E+00	0.000E+00	-4.19	3.343E+04	3.998E+04

Fires

Compartment	Fire	Plume Flow (kg/s)	Pyrol Rate (kg/s)	Fire Size (W)	Flame Height (m)	Fire in Upper (W)	Fire in Lower (W)	Vent Fire (W)	Convec. (W)	Radiat. (W)
	Main	1.57	5.409E-02	1.047E+06	3.31				7.328E+05	3.140E+05
1		1.57	5.409E-02	1.047E+06		1.353E-10	1.047E+06	0.000E+00		

Surfaces and Targets

Compartment	Ceiling Temp. (K)	Up wall Temp. (K)	Low wall Temp. (K)	Floor Temp. (K)	Target	Target Temp. (K)	Flux To Target (W/m^2)	Fire Rad. (%)	Surface Rad. (%)	Gas Rad. (%)	Convect. (%)
1	845.0	849.2	857.9	909.0	Floor	909.	3.9982E+04	0.0	58.4	24.1	17.6

Upper Layer Species

Compartment	N2 (%)	O2 (%)	CO2 (%)	CO (ppm)	HCN (ppm)	HCL (ppm)	TUHC (%)	H2O (%)	OD (1/m)	HCl c (mg/m^2)	HCl f (mg/m^2)	HCl uw (mg/m^2)	HCl lw (mg/m^2)
1	76.1	14.8	4.31	2.031E+03	0.000	0.000	0.000	4.11	2.77	0.000	0.000	0.000	0.000

Lower Layer Species

Compartment	N2 (%)	O2 (%)	CO2 (%)	CO (ppm)	HCN (ppm)	HCL (ppm)	TUHC (%)	H2O (%)	OD (1/m)	HCl c (mg/m^2)	HCl f (mg/m^2)	HCl uw (mg/m^2)	HCl lw (mg/m^2)
1	78.9	20.1	0.483	228.	0.000	0.000	0.000	0.461	0.623	0.000	0.000	0.000	0.000

Flow Through Vents (kg/s)

To Compartment	Through Vent	Upper Layer Inflow (Kg/s)	Upper Layer Outflow (Kg/s)	Lower Layer Inflow (Kg/s)	Lower Layer Outflow (Kg/s)	Mixing To Upper (Kg/s)	Mixing To Lower (Kg/s)
1	H Outside #1			6.890E-03			
	H Outside #2		6.662E-03				
	H Outside #3		1.40	1.34			0.170
Outside	H Comp 1 #1				6.890E-03		
	H Comp 1 #2	6.662E-03					
	H Comp 1 #3	1.40			1.34		

Interior Wall Temperature Profiles

Compartment	Wall	Temp. (K)	Temp. (K)	Temp. (K)	Temp. (K)	Temp. (K)	Temp. (K)	Temp. (K)	Temp. (K)	Temp. (K)	Temp. (K)
1	Ceiling	845.0	844.9	844.7	844.4	844.0	843.4	842.8	842.0	841.1	840.0
		838.9	837.6	836.2	834.6	833.0	831.2	829.3	827.3	825.2	823.0
		820.6	731.1	657.5	598.2	551.1	514.5	487.1	468.1	456.8	453.1
1	Up wall	849.2	849.1	848.9	848.6	848.2	847.6	847.0	846.2	845.3	844.2
		843.1	841.8	840.4	838.9	837.3	835.5	833.7	831.7	829.6	827.3
		825.0	736.3	663.4	604.6	558.1	522.0	495.1	476.3	465.3	461.6
1	Low wall	857.9	857.8	857.6	857.3	856.9	856.3	855.7	854.9	854.0	852.9
		851.8	850.5	849.1	847.6	845.9	844.2	842.3	840.3	838.2	835.9
		833.6	744.1	670.4	610.7	563.3	526.4	498.8	479.6	468.3	464.5
1	Floor	909.0	908.9	908.8	908.5	908.1	907.6	907.0	906.3	905.4	904.5
		903.4	902.3	901.0	899.6	898.1	896.5	894.8	893.0	891.1	889.0
		886.9	794.4	715.7	649.7	595.5	552.1	518.9	495.4	481.4	476.7

Tenability Measures

Compartment	FED1	FED2	FED3	TEMP1	TEMP2	Ct	Flux
1	7.747E-02	2.59	0.245	602.	3.530E+05	0.000E+00	1.789E+04

171

Appendix C Using CPlot

The CFAST model provides 3-D pictorial results and graphs while the model is executing. The model predicts the environment produced by a fire in one of several compartments, and follows smoke and toxic gases from one compartment to another, separately predicting values for each of the variables in both the upper and lower layers. The results of these calculations are written to a special data file (the "history" file) at designated time steps. CPlot is intended to provide a visual interface to generate graphs and tables from the time histories saved by the model. CPlot has the capability to form a list of variables, read in their values at each time interval, list the values in tabular form, plot the values, and save the variables in a formatted file for use with other software. In addition, it has the capability to read history files created by other programs to plot along with CFAST data. It can read these files for several runs of each program and combine them into one or more plots and lists. To start CPlot enter the command:

```
cplot
```

Once the CPlot command line has been entered, identifying information and a "command prompt" are displayed. Commands to direct the generation of the tables and graphs may now be entered. Commands available at the "command prompt" are:

> ADD, DELETE
> AGAIN
> CLEAR
> DEFAULT
> DIRECTORY
> END
> HELP
> FILE, ASCII, RAPID, TENAB
> LIST
> PLOT, REPLOT
> READ
> REVIEW
> SAVE
> SHIFT
> VARIABLE

These commands can be broken into five major groups that describe the process used to generate tabular or graphical output with CPlot. Each command has a sub-menu from which specific choices are made or actions taken. The following is a description of each of the commands. At least three characters must be used to identify a command.

173

C.1 Entering Data Into CPlot

The general procedure for using CPlot is to select the data from one or more files, then plot or print the data. The first step involves selecting the file. CPlot can currently read four types of data files:

- data created by the CFAST model (CFAST history files),

- data created by the TENAB model (TENAB history files)

- data created in specially formatted ASCII text files from other programs including RAPID, a program developed by the Building and Fire Research Laboratory for analysis of large-scale fire tests, and

- ASCII text files, with data which is blank delimited.

The command for reading each of these file types is FILE, TENAB, RAPID, or ASCII, respectively. Variables for the TENAB, RAPID, and ASCII file types are specified at the same time as the command. For the CFAST history file, variables are selected with the ADD command. In addition to the file type and variable selection commands, several utility commands are available to provide support for data entry.

FILE   Allows the user to specify the CFAST history file name. To select particular variables from a selected history file, use the ADD command.

TENAB   Reads a file in the TENAB format. The TENAB program produces estimates for a number of tenability criteria for persons exposed to a fire environment predicted by the CFAST model. The user must enter the "person number" and the desired criteria to be read from the file. The possibilities are:

Tenab Variable List
1.   Fractional Effective Dose Due to Gases - Bukowski
2.   Fractional Effective Dose Due to Gases - Purser
3.   Fractional Effective Dose Due to CO2 - Purser
4.   Temperature - Deg C
5.   Fractional Effective Dose Due to Convective Heat
6.   CT (G-MIN/M3)
7.   Flux (KW-MIN/M2)
8.   Derksen Curve

RAPID   Reads a file in the RAPID format after querying for the channels to read.
                 In order for this to work, there must be a channel which corresponds to the
                 default channel as selected by the DEFAULT command. Normally this is
                 the time channel, but it can be any other desired channel.

ASCII   Reads a file in columnar ASCII format after querying for the columns to
                 read. In order for this to work, there must be a column which corresponds
                 to the default column as selected by the DEFAULT command. Normally
                 this is the time, but it can be any other desired column.

If a CFAST history file has been specified using the FILE command, variables must then be
selected with the ADD command. The variables currently available are:

boundary surface temperature (ceiling, floor)	WALL	C
entrained mass flow in the plume	ENTRAIN	kg/s
hcl wall surface concentration	HCL	kg/m^2
heat release in lower layer	LPLUME	kW
heat release in upper layer	UPLUME	kW
heat release in flame out a vent	VFIRE	kW
heat release rate of the fire	HEAT	kW
layer height	INTE	m
layer temperature	TEMP	C
layer mass density	MASS	kg/m^3
mass flow from the plume into the upper layer	PLUME	kg/s
pyrolysis rate of the fuel	PYROL	kg/s
pressure	PRES	Pa
radiation field to a target	TARGET	W/m^2
species density	SPECIES	
total radiative heat flux into the layer	RAD	W
total convective heat flux into the layer	CONVEC	W
vent flow	VENT	kg/s
vent entrainment	JET	kg/s
volume of the upper layer	VOLUME	m^3

ADD   This command is used to build a list of CFAST variables to be read into the active list. This command applies only to files selected with the FILE command. ADD may be entered by itself or together with a list of variables that are to be added. If it is entered alone, the variables that are to be added to the list are requested. For example:

> ADD
        - INPUT VARIABLES TO BE ADDED>TEMP,PRES

or

> ADD TEMP,PRES

For each variable selected, a series of questions are displayed in order to identify exactly the type of variable desired. One question displayed for all variables is:

WHICH COMPARTMENT? ->

For layer dependent variables, the user is requested to input the layer (U for upper or L for lower):

WHICH LAYER? ->

The current default value is assumed for each question when the Enter key is pressed without providing a response to the prompt. See the DEFAULT command to change these default values.

If the VENTFLOW variable is chosen, the compartments of origin and destination are requested along with the vent number. If the SPECIES variable is selected, the species name (O_2, CO_2,...) is requested.

The maximum number of variables allowed in the active list at any one time is 40. If the list is full or the variable is currently in the active list, the addition is disallowed, and control returns to the CPlot command prompt.

The AGAIN, CLEAR, DELETE, READ, and REVIEW commands allow the user to view and manipulate the list of variables read with the data entry commands.

AGAIN	Repeats the input of a list of variables for a new CFAST history file. CPlot maintains a list of the most recently acquired CFAST variables. As an example, select a file with the FILE command, and select a set of variables. Now use the FILE command again to select a new file. Enter the AGAIN command to select the original list of variables for this new file. This function simplifies direct comparisons between runs of CFAST. It works only with files selected with the FILE command.
CLEAR	Empties the current variable list.
DELETE	When this command is entered, the current list of CFAST variables is displayed on the screen. The user is asked to select the variables to delete by entering the associated number from the list. The variables must be entered on a single line separated by commas or blanks. If the variable number entered does not correspond to one currently on the list, it is ignored. After the deletions have been completed, a new list is displayed. If the list is currently empty, an appropriate error message is displayed. One caution concerning order. The variables are deleted by the associated number in the list, not by rank ordering within the group. This is important in conjunction with use of the AGAIN command.
READ	Used to force a read of the data files. This is most useful for script files which can be processed automatically to display data. It is equivalent to pressing an enter at the "read prompt" in the interactive mode.
REVIEW	At times, the user may wish to view the current list before entering a command. This may be done with the REVIEW command. It prints out the current list along with the compartment number, species, and layer specified for each of the variables.

C.2 Generating Tables and Graphs With CPlot

Once the data has been selected and read, CPlot can plot or print the data values. The commands LIST and PLOT allow the user to generate a table of values or a graph for selected variables. The SHIFT command allows the user to shift the abscissa (horizontal) or ordinate (vertical) axis of a variable.

LIST   Lists the values of any of the variables in the current list to the screen. The variables desired and the time range for the list are requested. Once the list is displayed on the screen, it can be printed with the PRINT SCREEN key.

PLOT   After entering the PLOT command, the current list of variables is displayed. To group variables together for a single graph use parentheses. Separate variables within the parentheses by commas or blank spaces. Variables to be plotted together on a single graph must be of the same type. As an example:

```
Select 1->4 graphs by grouping variables
with parentheses followed by a return >(1 2 3 4)
```

will plot 1 graph with 4 variables to the screen,

while:

```
Select 1->4 graphs by grouping variables
with parentheses followed by a return >1,2,3,4
```

or

```
Select 1->4 graphs by grouping variables
with parentheses followed by a return >1 2 3 4
```

plots 4 graphs of 1 variable each to the screen.

Normally, CPlot will scale the axes automatically. However, if the automatic formatting option has been turned off using the DEFAULT command, the user is given the opportunity to change the range of the X and Y axes along with the graph legends before the graph is drawn. The maximum and minimum values for the X and Y axes are displayed followed by a request for any changes. Press enter if no change is desired. The next axis change request is displayed:

```
The Min/Max for Temperature  are:
X =        0.00 TO     2000.00
Y =        0.00 TO     1000.00

<ENTER> If no changes are desired.
      Xmin =          0.00, Change to =
      Xmax =       2000.00, Change to =
      Ymin =          0.00, Change to =
      Ymax =       1000.00, Change to =
```

Similar prompts are made for the legends for each graph. The user is allowed to change the text for each curve label and the position. If no changes are desired, the Enter key may be pressed to accept the suggested values for the legend text and position:

```
Legend for  1 (Temperature  1 U  ) is |R 1 U|. :
<ENTER> For no change:
Legend for  2 (Temperature  2 U  ) is |R 2 U|. :
<ENTER> For no change:

Legend for graph 1 is at X=      40.00, Y=     945.49
<ENTER> If no changes are desired.
      X =       40.00, Change to =
      Y =      945.49, Change to =
```

When all changes have been made, the selected graphs are plotted.

SHIFT Used to adjust the variable axes. For example, it may be used when plotting variables from different files to normalize the data to a common ignition time or initial temperature. The required input is a selection of the axis to shift, the amount of shift, and a list of channels. Please note that shifting the time axis for a single variable will shift the time axis for all variables associated with that particular file. Such an effect occurs because only one vector of values is kept to represent the timeline for each file.

C.3 Saving Data With CPlot

The SAVE command allows the user to create an ASCII text file in one of two formats. These files may be used for future CPlot runs or for exporting CFAST or TENAB data to other programs.

SAVE   Saves the values for the variables in the current list into a file. The format used depends on the option chosen by the DEFAULT command. Columnar data can be used for spreadsheet and charting programs. Row data is used to make the data compatible with the data processing program (RAPID) designed for the reduction of experimental data in the Building and Fire Research Laboratory.

The user is prompted for the file name. A verification is made to determine if the file currently exists. If the file does exist, the user is asked if the new data should write over the old file. If the response is NO, no data is stored in the file. If the response is YES or the file does not already exist, the file is created, and the data stored.

Columnar data files are straightforward with each variable listed. The time channel is the first column.

For files in the row format, each variable in the list is saved with the following line at the beginning of each block of data:

I6,I6,A6,*-----------COMMENT----------

The first I6 represents the number of data points for that variable, the next I6 specifies the number given to that variable on the list, and the A6 is the actual variable name. Everything after the "*" is a comment block and contains information relevant to that particular variable, such as species number, compartment number, layer, etc. The actual numerical data is written using the format 7E11.5.

C.4 Changing the Default Parameters in CPlot

The DEFAULT command allows the user to change a number of default parameters within CPlot. These defaults include the format of the graphical output along with values assumed by CPlot when the user presses the Enter key without specifying input.

DEFAULT   Enables the user to set default parameters for the following:

Default compartment specifies the compartment number to be used whenever the user presses an Enter in response to a question requesting a compartment number. Ventflow destination specifies the compartment number for the "to compartment" for vent flows. Default species and default layer specify the species and layer, respectively, to be used whenever the user presses an Enter in response to a request for a species or a layer. Character set is a number from 1 to 25 which specifies a different typeface to be used. Only character sets 4, 7, 24, and 25 are supplied with CFAST. Graphics device specifies where the graphic output is placed. Allowable outputs are type 1 or SCREEN for output to the screen, and type 6 or HPGL for output to a file formatted for Hewlett-Packard format devices. Automatic plot formatting allows the user to customize the format of the graphical output. A response of Yes instructs CPlot to format the axes and legends automatically. A response of No allows the user to select the axis limits and legend text manually for each plot. Channel for abscissa specifies the channel number to be used for the horizontal axis for data read from RAPID format data files with the RAPID command. Factor for abscissa specifies the data column number to be used for the horizontal axis for data read in ASCII format. Type of save file specifies the format of the file written by the SAVE command. Finally, Draw curves in color (Y/N) and Draw curves with dashed lines (Y/N), allow the user to customize the lines to be drawn for each variable in a plot.

The defaults are saved in a permanent file on the disk so the next execution of CPlot will use the defaults most recently selected.

C.5 Getting Online Help in CPlot

The HELP and VARIABLE commands provide some simple online help when using CPlot.

HELP   This command may be entered any time the user is prompted for an option. The purpose is to list to the screen the available commands with a brief explanation of each. After listing the commands, another option is requested.

VARIABLE   Shows the list of variables which are available for the files selected with the FILE command (CFAST history files). This list is identical to the one shown in the introduction to this CPlot section.

DIRECTORY   Shows a list of files in the current (or remote if set) directory. Functions in a manner similar to the "dir" ("ls" in Unix) command. Wildcards are used in the usual fashion.

C.6 Exiting CPlot

The END command terminates the execution of CPlot. If desired, any data which has been read into CPlot should be saved prior to entering this command. Any data not saved is lost upon exiting CPlot and must be re-entered if it is to be used again.

Appendix D CFAST Thermal Properties Database Format

Thermal data is read from a file which is in an ASCII format. The default name is THERMAL.DF. An alternative can be chosen by using the key word THRMF in the data file that is used by the CFAST model.

The relationship is by the name used in specifying the boundary. Any name can be used so long as it is in the thermal database. If a name is used which is not in the database, then FAST will turn off the conduction calculation, and FAST will stop with an appropriate error message. The form of an entry in the database is:

name conductivity specific heat density thickness emissivity

and the units are:

name	1 to 8 alphanumeric characters
conductivity	Watts/meter/Kelvin
specific heat	Joules/kilogram/Kelvin
density	kilograms/cubic meter
thickness	meters
emissivity	dimensionless.

Appendix E CFAST Object Fire Database Format

The object database was modified to handle the new definition of a flame spread object. The opportunity was taken to create an general format for an API so that all databases (thermal, objects, ...) can be read by a sumilar set of routines in CFAST, CEdit, CLite and so on. Please note that the format for the objects database for CFAST 2.2 (and earlier) and 3.0 are not compatible.

line 1) OBJECT OBJNAM

      OBJNAM(NUMOBJL) = Name of object (up to 8 characters)

line 2) OBJTYP OBJCRI(2,I) OBJCRI(3,I) OBJMAS OBJGMW OBJVT OBJHC

      OBJTYP(NUMOBJL) = Object type
         1 unconstrained burn
         2 constrained burn
         3 flame spread model
      OBJCRI(2,NUMOBJL) = Flux for ignition (w/m^2)
      OBJCRI(3,NUMOBJL) = Surface temperature for ignition (k)
      OBJMAS(NUMOBJL)　= Total mass (kg)
      OBJGMW(NUMOBJL)　= Gram molecular weight
      OBJVT(NUMOBJL)　= Volatilization temperature (k)
      OBJHC(NUMOBJL)　= Heat of combustion (J/kg)

line 3) OBJXYZ(1,I) OBJXYZ(2,I) OBJXYZ(3,I) OBJORT(1,I) OBJORT(2,I) OBJORT(3,I)

      OBJXYZ(1,NUMOBJL) = Panel length (m)
      OBJXYZ(2,NUMOBJL) = Panel height or width (m)
      OBJXYZ(3,NUMOBJL) = Panel thickness (m)
      OBJORT(1,NUMOBJL) = x component of the normal
      OBJORT(2,NUMOBJL) = y component of the normal
      OBJORT(3,NUMOBJL) = z component of the normal

For type 1 and 2 fires line 4) is blank. For type 3 objects line 4 has data specific only to flame spread. The format for a flame spread object follows.

line 4) OBJMINT OBJPHI OBJHGAS OBJQAREA

OBJMINT = Minimum surface temperature for lateral flame spread (K)
OBJPHI = Lateral flame spread parameter (J^2/s^2*m^3)
OBJHGAS = Effective heat of gasification (J/kg)
OBJQAREA   = Total heat per unit area (J/m^2)

The effective heat of gasification is the one unusual parameter for the flame spread object. The method given by Quintiere and Cleary is to plot the peak heat release rate (HRR) against the radiant flux used for a number of cone calorimeter runs at different fluxes. The slope of the curve that bests fits the data is the effective heat of gasification.

line 5) OTIME(1,I) to OTIME(TOTJ,I)

OTIME(NV,NUMOBJL) = Time history (sec)

Each OTIME(J,I) represents a point on the objects burn time line where the variables below are defined exactly. CFAST will interpolate values between any two points. TOTJ is the total number of points on the specified time line. CFAST automatically assigns an initial time zero for the objects time line so that there will always be one fewer specified value for the time line than for the history variables below. For type three objects the curves are straight lines to represent the constants that CFAST uses for the flame spread objects.

The following lines are the histories for the individual parameters at each of the OTIME points.

Line 6) OMASS(1,I) to OMASS(TOTJ+1,I)

OMASS(NV,NUMOBJL) = Pyrolysis rate time history (kg/sec)

line 7) OQDOT(1,I) to OQDOT(TOTJ,I)

OQDOT(NV,NUMOBJL) = Rate of heat release time history (w)

line 8) OAREA(1,I) to OAREA(TOTJ,I)

OAREA(NV,NUMOBJL) = Area of fire time history (m^2)

line 9) OHIGH(1,I) to OHIGH(TOTJ,I)

OHIGH(NV,NUMOBJL) = Height of flame time history (m)

line 10) OCO(1,NUMOBJL) to OCO(TOTJ,NUMOBJL)

OCO(NV,NUMOBJL) = CO/CO2 time history

line 11) OOD(1,NUMOBJL) to OOD(TOTJ,NUMOBJL)

OOD(NV,NUMOBJL) = OD or soot time history

line 12) OHRC(1,NUMOBJL) to OHRC(TOTJ,NUMOBJL)

OHCR(NV,NUMOBJL) = H/C time history

line 13) OOC(1,I) to OOC(TOTJ,I)

OOC(NV,NUMOBJL) = O/C time history

line 14) OMPRODR(1,10,I) to OMPRODR(TOTJ,10,I)

OMPRODR(NV,10,NUMOBJL) = CT time history

line 15) OMPRODR(1,5,I) to OMPRODR(TOTJ,5,I)

OMPRODR(NV,5,NUMOBJL) = HCN time history

line 16) OMPRODR(1,6,I) to OMPRODR(TOTJ,6,I)

OMPRODR(NV,6,NUMOBJL) = HCl time history

Index